CLIPPER
SHIPS
AND THE GOLDEN
AGE OF SAIL

CLIPPER SHIPS

AND THE GOLDEN
AGE OF SAIL

RACES AND RIVALRIES ON THE
NINETEENTH CENTURY HIGH SEAS

Published by Adlard Coles Nautical
an imprint of Bloomsbury Publishing Plc
50 Bedford Square, London WC1B 3DP
www.adlardcoles.com

Bloomsbury is a trademark of Bloomsbury Publishing Plc

First published by Adlard Coles Nautical in 2014

ISBN 978-1-4729-0028-9
ePDF 978-1-4729-0030-2
ePub 978-1-4729-0029-6

A CIP catalogue record for this book is available from the British Library.

This book is produced using paper that is made from wood grown in managed, sustainable forests. It is natural, renewable and recyclable. The logging and manufacturing processes conform to the environmental regulations of the country of origin.

Typeset in Haarlemmer MT 11pt
Printed and bound in China by C&C Offset Printing Co.

10 9 8 7 6 5 4 3 2

CONTENTS

INTRODUCTION   VII

1 THE ORIGINS OF CLIPPER SHIPS   1
Baltimore clippers   2
Britain lags behind   5
Gold rush   6
Time for tea   12
Beauty at any cost   16
End of an era   20

2 A HELL SHIP VOYAGE WITH 'BULLY' WATERMAN   23
Fame and fortune   24
A challenge for the *Challenge*   29
Rotten crew   32
Crisis at Cape Horn   40
The reckoning in San Francisco   41
The aftermath   47

3 *MARCO POLO*, THE FASTEST SHIP IN THE WORLD 49
A stranding with a twist   50
Under new ownership   55
Up through the hawse-pipe   55
Troubles on the record passage   57
Commander of the *Lightning*   60
The *Schomberg*'s only voyage   69
Dangerous gamble   71
Decline and fall   73

4 MARY PATTEN'S BATTLE WITH CAPE HORN   81
The *Rapid*'s turnaround   83
An unusual honeymoon   85
Captain and mate   89
Mary's dilemma   91
Keeler's second chance   92
The frustrating final leg   97
End of the fairytale   100

**5 MUTINY ABOARD THE 'WILD BOAT
    OF THE ATLANTIC'   103**
The *Dreadnought*'s recipe
    for success   105
Liverpool packet rats   109
The provocation   111
Crisis point   117
Rudderless in mid-ocean   121
Wrecked near Cape Horn   125

6 THE GREAT CHINA TEA RACE OF 1866   127
Out to sea   129
The captains and their ships   132
The challenges of sailing
    China clippers   137
Manoeuvring for position   143
On the home stretch   150

7 THE *SIR LANCELOT* DEFIES THE ODDS   159
Dismasted in the Bay of Biscay   160
The race line-up   163
'Go ahead' Robinson   168
The *Sir Lancelot* catches up   168
A new rival   171
Against the *Thermopylae*   179
Robinson's final record   181

8 THE *CUTTY SARK*'S LONGEST VOYAGE   185
Cruel mate   190
Search for a new skipper   193
Tramp of the ocean   199
Hazing and hardship   202
Drunk in command   203
Wool clipper   206

EPILOGUE
Twilight   213

APPENDIX
Principal records set by British
and American clipper ships   221

CREDITS   226

INDEX   229

INTRODUCTION

From a very early age I was utterly obsessed with ships and the sea. Bearing in mind that I come from a particularly landlocked part of Cumbria, no one in my family could really account for it. They looked on with bemused interest as I spent my days up in trees pretending it was the rigging of a ship or floating pieces of wood down the river that ran by our house in order to recreate some race or naval battle. At first my nautical obsession was very general, although I always favoured sail over power, but at the age of 12 my interest was put sharply into focus when I received a book entitled *Clipper Ships* by David R MacGregor. I read the book with my usual interest until I reached the following passage. A recollection by Frederick Paton, who had served as midshipman aboard the tea clipper *Flying Spur;* after grumbling a good deal about how his captain did not drive her hard enough, he proceeded thus:

'One morning Flying Spur *was snoring through the NE, trades under all sail to royal staysails, with her lower yards just touching the backstays. At 11.20 am a sail was sighted on the horizon ahead. This proved to be the Glasgow clipper,* Lochleven Castle, *80 days out from Rangoon to Liverpool. At 1 pm the* Flying Spur *was up with her, and as we went foaming by, the* Lochleven Castle's *main topgallant sail went to ribbons with a clap of thunder, and her mainsail split from top to bottom; at the same moment our cook with all his pots and pans was washed from the galley to the break of the poop. An hour and a half later the* Lochleven Castle *was out of sight astern.'*

I was hooked; there is so much drama, excitement and beauty in that one paragraph, that one jubilant morning when two ships were pushed to their absolute limit for the sheer sport of the race that I simply wanted to know more. I was delighted to discover that over the span of 20 years these beautiful ships were raced across the oceans and their adventures were more compelling than any fiction.

Before starting this book, it is important to clear up exactly what a clipper was; there are many out there that think that any vessel setting square sails is a clipper. This is not so. Clippers were

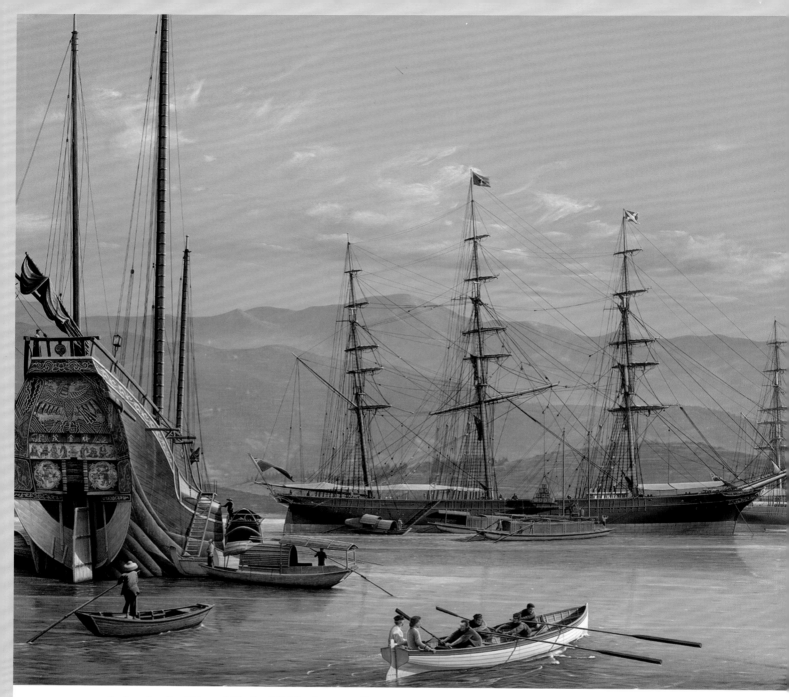

Lying in the River Min in 1869, the tea clippers *Ariel*, *Thermopylae* and *Serica* await their tea cargoes.

commercial vessels built with speed as the foremost consideration and cargo carrying secondary. This meant that her hull must be very sharp. Clippers in their purest form were only built between 1845 and 1875. After that date, they made way for the lordly tall ships, 'windjammers', as they were somewhat scornfully labelled by those obsessed with the relentless progress associated with the turn of the steamship's screw. Some of these old timers still work as sail training vessels or are preserved as museum ships in the various corners of the globe

which they eventually washed up in. These vessels have their own grandeur, but none of the grace of the clipper ships, which were little more than yachts of large tonnage. As an example, the tea clipper, *Leander* was launched in 1868 and was so sharp that her hold could not be filled before her load line was underwater. This was not practical, but her lines were irresistible and somehow that was more important.

As I grew older I took to the sea myself and it was here that I fully realised what we had lost. Picture, if you will, a perfectly proportioned clipper, all

graceful overhangs and shining brass; bigger sister to the gleamingly preserved classic yachts that still gather off St Tropez and La Spezia every summer. Her master and crew could handle the vessel with an easy skill that we can barely conceive now. If a clipper was beautiful at rest, under sail she came alive, flying before a gale, skimming before the trade winds or ghosting through calms. Contrast this with a modern cargo vessel, plodding across the world, punching against the seas, a trail of oil and smoke in her wake, a slave to her motor and a relentless schedule. I can't help but feel that something vital has been lost in this quest for efficiency.

Now the clipper ships have long passed on and the world is just a fraction less beautiful and exciting as a result. All that this book seeks to do, both through the pictures and text, is to celebrate the skill and tenacity of the men who handled these ships, enjoy the remarkable beauty of the vessels themselves and cherish the rarity of what they symbolise; something we humans have created that is in harmony with nature rather than at odds with it.

CHAPTER ONE

THE ORIGINS OF CLIPPER SHIPS

The philanthropist William Morris once said that there could be no true beauty without purpose. His words seem to encapsulate something that lay at the very heart of the clipper ship era. The 20 years between 1850 and 1870 saw the launch of several hundred ships designed to carry small amounts of cargo at very high speeds. Although all these vessels had a practical purpose, they were also utterly beautiful; white sails curved like petals, their gleaming hulls low and sleek. The sight of such a vessel racing along at 15 knots and more, coppered hull gleaming in the light and smothered in white spray as she leant purposefully into the waves, could inspire even the least romantic sailor to bouts of poetic musing. Their feats were celebrated and eulogised long after they were gone. Now their magic is fading and their exploits and daring masters are almost forgotten. This book is an endeavour to evoke the memory of these beautiful vessels and the mighty characters who commanded them.

The clipper ship era began in earnest in 1845, when the brand-new ship *Rainbow* lay on the stocks of Smith and Dimon's New York shipyard. Designed by the young naval architect John W Griffiths, she displayed some innovative features that left many observers bewildered. 'Why, she looks as if she's been turned inside out!' was the general comment as they observed her very sharp, concave bow lines. The *Rainbow* represented the polar opposite of accepted ship design, which favoured a bluff, barrel-shaped bow in order to give a ship buoyancy as she pounded into a head sea. Meanwhile, others

A group of opium clippers lying off Lintin, Hong Kong. The opium clippers were the predecessors of the true clipper ships and were used to smuggle opium into China from India. This was a high risk, high stakes trade and the ships had to be fast to avoid pirates and the Chinese authorities.

stared in horror at her tall spars and narrow hull, stating that she would roll over before she had left New York Harbour.

Despite these dire predictions, the new vessel raced out to China and back in a little over six months. Any ships she encountered on her voyage were rapidly overhauled and sunk below the horizon. She was the first of a new breed, a line of clipper ships whose voyages and exploits were to prove the very zenith of the commercial sailing ship. The leisurely vessels that had been gradually evolving since the era of Columbus and before were swept aside by this radical new design that could not only consistently sail 300 nautical miles and more a day, but was also capable of sailing efficiently to windward.

Baltimore clippers

Prior to the 1840s, rapid sailing ships were generally small fry – privateer brigs, slavers and opium smugglers. Many of these vessels originated in Baltimore and it was here that the term 'clipper' was first coined. Some believe it was because they ran at a fair 'clip'; others think it was because they 'clipped' a few days off the usual passage time. The Baltimore clippers were generally schooner-rigged with tall, heavily raked spars, and they presented a very dashing sight at sea, one that often wrought fear into the hearts of honest traders.

Yet their design was evolutionary rather than revolutionary. It wasn't until the arrival of the *Rainbow* that a larger, more radical vessel was launched featuring sharp, hollow bow lines and a narrow hull. The main driving force behind this desire to innovate was American merchants who had seen the financial benefits of getting goods back from China quickly. The ship that brought back the first crop of tea from China commanded the best price and merchants started to develop faster vessels such as the *Houqua*, built in 1844. From here, it only took a small leap of imagination from John Griffiths to produce the first full-blown clipper ship, the *Rainbow*.

The *Sylph* was one of the most successful of these early opium clippers and is seen here in the China Sea. She was built in 1831 for an Indian Parsee. She carried a crew of 70 and was heavily armed.

The *Shenandoah*, a modern day replica of a Baltimore clipper.

By 1850 it was evident that American clippers were seriously outclassing their leisurely British rivals and the superiority of American design was further underlined when the yacht *America* visited the UK and put the cream of the British fleet to the sword in the 100 Guineas Cup, inaugurating the America's Cup in the process. Here she is seen on her sea trials in New York Harbour.

The East Indiaman *Malabar*. The design of such vessels was the culmination of centuries of evolutionary design which was blown away by the clipper ship revolution. Vessels such as the *Malabar* would rarely be able to sail at over nine knots and were very poor at sailing to windward.

The *Oriental* arriving triumphant in London Docks loaded with tea. Her 97-day passage was far faster than any British ship had managed before.

Britain lags behind

Meanwhile in Britain, old-fashioned attitudes and a lack of competition stymied the development of fast ships. The Navigation Act was partly to blame as it meant that only British-owned ships could trade with Britain and the British East India Company almost completely controlled trade with the Far East and India. Only their ships could carry goods back home to Britain. With no competition, complacency was rife and vessels tended to come home in very leisurely times, with stale goods to sell at top prices.

In 1849, the Navigation Act was repealed in favour of free trade. Suddenly the faster American vessels could sail to London and they duly demonstrated how far advanced they were compared with their British rivals. Things reached a head in 1850 when the Yankee clipper *Oriental* turned up in London after a 97-day passage from Canton.

She commanded huge prices for the tea cargo she had brought to the market many months before her more leisurely rivals. British ship owners wrung their hands in despair. The superiority of

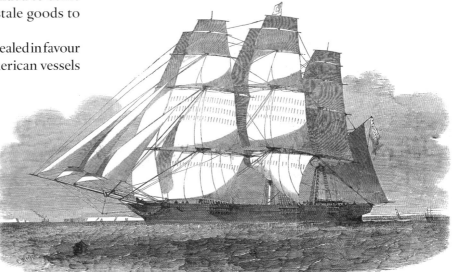

The American clipper *Oriental* caused despair in England after racing from China to London in record time.

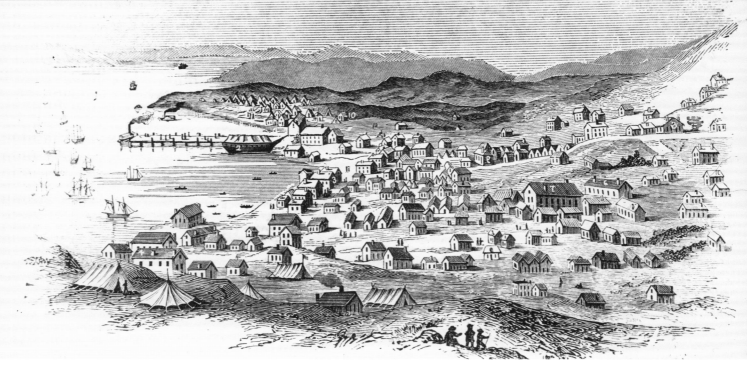

This painting of San Francisco in 1849 shows the gold rush town already crowded with ships.

the Americans was further emphasised when the schooner *America* humiliated the entire Royal Yacht Squadron during her epoch-making race around the Isle of Wight in 1851.

Gold rush
Yet by this time, undercutting the British tea ships had become small beer to the Americans; they had much bigger matters on their mind. In 1849 gold was discovered at Sutter's Mill in northern California. For the next couple of years hysteria reigned as a general stampede ensued to get to San Francisco and the gold fields beyond.

In 1834, Richard Dana paid a visit to San Francisco in the American ship *Alert*. He described a tranquil and very beautiful wooded bay with only one other ship riding at anchor. There were almost no houses. By 1850 gold had changed all that. The bay was now dominated by a great rambling shanty town of rough tents and adobe houses, with a main street lined with casinos and brothels. Every day new ships would anchor in the bay, their pumps working frantically to keep them afloat after the gruelling trip around Cape Horn. Entire crews, even captains, simply abandoned their ships as gold fever took hold, leaving the bay littered with derelict vessels.

Never before had a need for speed been so urgent. The easiest way to get goods to California was generally on a clipper ship sailing around Cape Horn. The overland route through the US was simply unfeasible at the time as there were no railroads. Travelling via Panama was also riddled with hazards and delays. Both these routes were untenable for shipping large quantities of goods. As San Francisco grew, demand for basic commodities also grew and the gold-rich prospectors were prepared to pay ludicrous prices for basics such as sugar, tea and clothes.

A ship built in New York and loaded with general cargo and passengers could clear the entire cost of being built in a single trip, and the shipyards of the US east coast were a frenzy of activity. Speed was the most important attribute, and designers were building more and more extreme vessels to cut the time of the voyage. Records tumbled almost daily: in 1850 the *Sea Witch* arrived in San Francisco, having made the passage in 97 days. From here on, it was just a question of time when a vessel would do the trip in under 90 days. Magnificent races occurred, with clippers arriving in 'Frisco' simultaneously after leaving New York on the same tide.

After racing out to San Francisco, these majestic vessels would generally cross to China, where they would ship tea to either New York or London. Here, they often put the British tea ships to the sword. Yet by 1851, the British were beginning to fight back. Led by the clever designs of Aberdeen shipbuilder Alexander Hall, the British were developing their

This image of one of the early paddle steamers shows how unsuitable they were for operating in heavy seas. Clipper ships were far more capable of riding out a storm in safety.

A prospector panning for gold.

Overleaf: The *Flying Cloud* running before a freshening breeze. This American clipper, built in 1851 by Donald McKay, was to prove one of the fastest of them all. On her maiden voyage she raced from New York to San Francisco in 89 days, a record which she equalled a couple of years later.

A selection of cards, used to advertise the sailing of a clipper from New York.

The *Robin Hood* was built in Aberdeen by Alexander Hall and was one of the improved British clippers that could rival the US clippers. She sailed in the China tea trade.

A contemporary painting of the Australian gold fields.

own clippers. These were generally much smaller than their American rivals and longer-lasting, built in hardwood as opposed to the light, flexible American softwoods, which tended to distort and become waterlogged after a few hard-driving voyages. The British clippers were not designed for rounding Cape Horn and were therefore generally daintier and often faster in light airs. By 1853, these smaller clippers were beginning to reassert British dominance on the tea trade.

The hysteria surrounding the gold rush was also dying down, and the demand for huge and very extreme clippers was coming to an end in the US. Yet the discovery of gold in Australia prompted a second gold rush and a number of extreme American clippers were launched for this trade.

These included three vessels built by Donald McKay of Boston: the *Lightning*, the *James Baines* and the *Champion of the Seas*. McKay was probably the leading American designer of the clipper ship era, and these vessels were bought by Liverpool ship owner James Baines and sent out to Australia. Their passages were rarely bettered and they excelled in the strong winds of the Southern Ocean. Skippers stated they could run at 22 knots and the *Champion of the Seas* claimed a record 24-hour run of 465 nautical miles. This is phenomenal running and many have disputed the veracity of these claims.

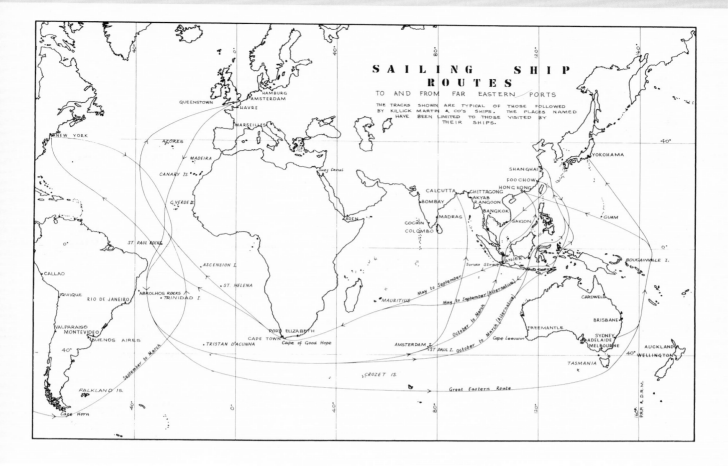

A map showing the principal trade routes followed by sailing ships in the 19th century.

Men out on the bowsprit taking in sail. At times this could be a very risky undertaking for a clipper ship. Her sharp bow was prone to plunging heavily in high seas and there was a very real danger of getting washed off.

However, these clippers were high-sided and lightly loaded and would have been able to withstand very heavy driving.

The Australian gold rush vessels marked the final stages of the American clipper ship era. By 1855, extreme clipper ship building in the US was at an end; the need for speed was bounded by a desire for good cargo-carrying capacities and shipbuilders started to compromise with more conservative designs. Meanwhile, the old clippers, badly strained from being thrashed around the Horn, were a shadow of their former selves and generally drifted into obscurity. The zenith of commercial sail in America was over. The Civil War of 1860 provided the final nail in the coffin.

Time for tea

Happily, this was not the end of the clipper ship era. It was the British obsession with tea that was to bring about one final and poetic flourish. The need to transport teas back from China as quickly as possible had ensured that fast little vessels continued to be launched from British yards throughout the 1850s. By the 1860s competition had started to intensify. Britain was a land of tea connoisseurs and Chinese tea was considered the finest of all. The first crop, picked in late April,

Different types of teas.

The big American clipper *Sovereign of the Seas* off San Francisco. The Australian gold rush extended the boom in American clipper shipbuilding, but not for long.

This chart of the South China Sea dates from 1801 and gives a good idea of the nightmarish labyrinth of shoals and rocks that littered the route home.

was of the highest quality but limited in quantity. Pekoe and Kaisow were two of the finest first crop teas and were hurried home by the very fastest tea clippers at the end of May.

The first ship home with new teas was guaranteed a high price and thus it became a race. In 1861 shippers introduced a £500 bonus for the first ship home and the race became official. By 1865, it was as closely followed as the Grand National or the Derby and just as hotly contested. Skippers would try any ruse to get ahead of their rivals. This was racing in the truest sense of the word. Forget modern yacht racing – to compare the two is like comparing BMX racing with the Tour de France. The captain of a clipper ship had up to 50 different sails to set on three masts. This created the sort of exacting work

that is almost unimaginable to the modern-day sailor. A successful racing captain had to expect to be deprived of sleep for weeks on end.

The risks were very real and navigation was sketchy at best as incomplete charts of the China Sea often left reefs unmarked. The contest between the British tea clipper *Chrysolite* and the American clipper *Memnon* in 1851 is an excellent example of the risks taken while racing. The two vessels had been company all the way down from Canton. As night fell on the evening of 23 June, the pair was approaching a narrow channel between Bangka and Pulo Leat. Captain Gordon of the *Memnon* was concerned and signalled the *Chrysolite* to ask if she was proceeding through. Her captain replied in the affirmative and the competitive

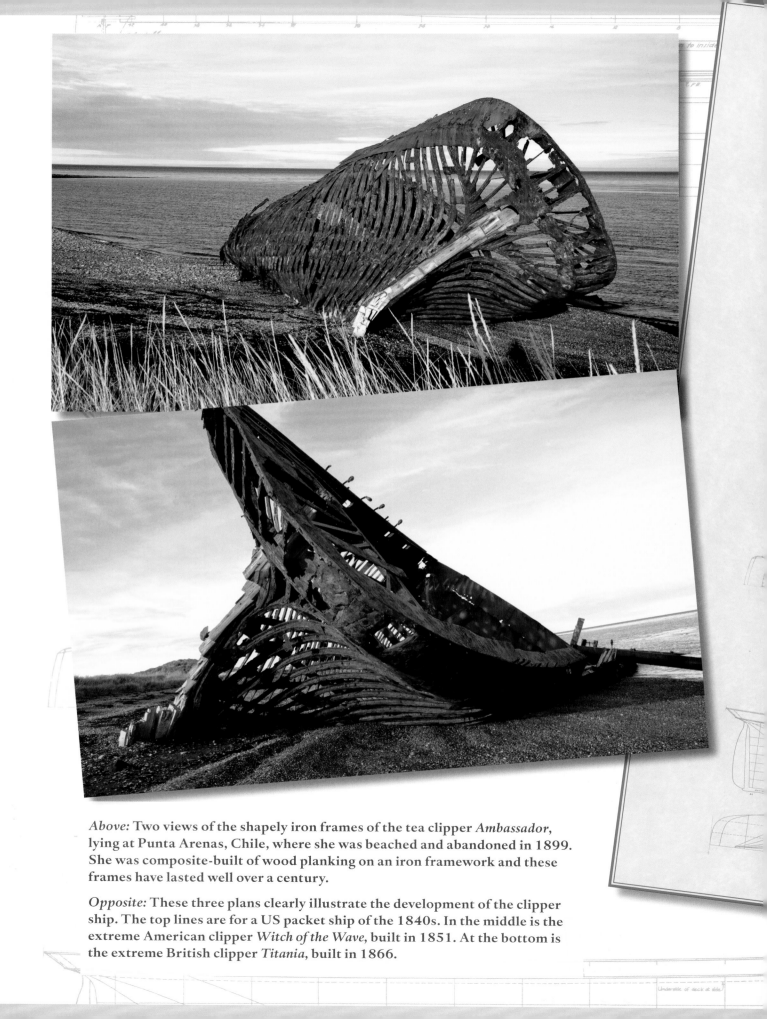

Above: Two views of the shapely iron frames of the tea clipper *Ambassador*, lying at Punta Arenas, Chile, where she was beached and abandoned in 1899. She was composite-built of wood planking on an iron framework and these frames have lasted well over a century.

Opposite: These three plans clearly illustrate the development of the clipper ship. The top lines are for a US packet ship of the 1840s. In the middle is the extreme American clipper *Witch of the Wave*, built in 1851. At the bottom is the extreme British clipper *Titania*, built in 1866.

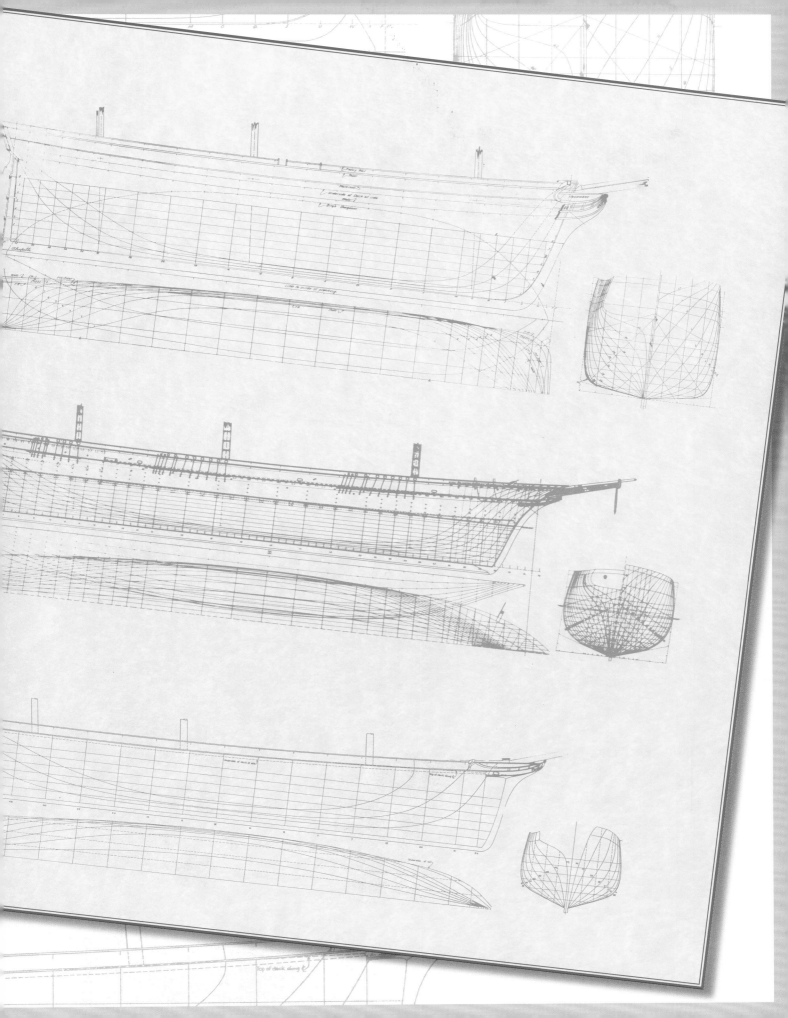

The River Clyde on a particularly clement summer day. More clippers were launched from shipyards along the banks of the Clyde than anywhere else in the world.

Gordon felt compelled to follow. Midway down this treacherous channel, the *Memnon* was struck by a squall and driven onto an uncharted reef. She was badly holed and in the morning Malay pirates boarded and stripped her. The ship was a total wreck and Captain Gordon was forced to abandon her. The endeavour to keep his boat in the race had cost him dearly.

Far daintier than their American cousins of the 1850s, the later British clippers were designed to sail very fast both to windward and in the light airs of the China Sea. The most successful clippers were able to ghost along with only the merest cat's paw to help them. It was often said of the very fast and successful clipper *Thermopylae* that she could run along at eight knots while her captain strolled the decks with a lit candle barely flickering in the breeze.

The majority of these vessels were launched from the Clyde yards of Glasgow and incorporated many new innovations. One of the major breakthroughs was composite construction. This method used the lightness and versatility of wooden planks but had the added benefit of a strong framework of iron ribs. This gave the vessels great strength and longevity.

Beauty at any cost

Aesthetics became a key feature and much attention was paid to ensuring that a vessel had a very graceful sheer. A yacht-like counter stern, cut away to the very maximum, was considered the height of elegance.

As the clipper fleet awaited the new season's tea in Foochow, a true show of beauty unfolded. Teak decks were scrubbed and sanded until they gleamed pure white and brass fittings and glossy black sides were polished. On the waterline, the copper sheathing used to protect the hull, usually green in port, was burnished until you could see your face in it. Only the crew of a modern classic yacht anchored idle off St Tropez can fully appreciate the kind of toil this entailed. Beauty was everything.

Perhaps the very epitome of this was the beautiful *Ariel*, built in 1865 in Greenock. One of the most successful tea clippers, she was noted for her elegant appearance and the comfort of the crew was severely compromised to achieve this. The deck was completely flush, featuring no raised poop deck at the stern and only a tiny deckhouse forward to cram in a crew of more than 30. Her bulwarks were also incredibly low, being only three feet high, and featured elegant painted panelling.

16

The beautiful *Ariel* under a heavy press of sail.

Overleaf: The *Taeping*, built in 1863 by Robert Steele of Greenock, was a typical tea clipper of the 1860s. She was probably the fastest ship in the trade between 1863 and 1866.

A depiction of the likely fate of the *Ariel* in 1872. Her stern was too fine and it is likely that she was pooped by a following sea, broached out of control, and was then pinned down on her beam ends and foundered.

The American 'Down Easter' *Thomas Reed* towing in to San Francisco Harbour. These later American clippers were built throughout the 1860s and were nowhere near as extreme as earlier vessels such as the *Flying Cloud*. They were named down easters as they were largely built in 'down east' ports such as Maine.

Brass was let in flush on the capping rail and was a nightmare to polish. This configuration left her very vulnerable in big following seas, when she was especially liable to having her decks swept clear.

Her yacht-like counter stern also provided very little buoyancy aft. Her captain, John Keay, wrote a vivid account of losing control of her in rough weather off the Cape of Good Hope. For several hours she was swept fore and aft and everything movable was hurled about the decks or overboard. The helmsman had to be lashed to the wheel to keep him in his rightful place. 'The ship ran away from me,' Keay later confided and admitted that for several hours all that could be done was hold on and hope for the best. It is telling that this same vessel later perished in the Southern Ocean while bound for Australia. Although no hands survived to tell the story, it is likely that she was simply overwhelmed by a big following sea.

The years 1863–69 saw some of the closest racing imaginable and new vessels would arrive on the scene every season to spice up the racing still further. Many of these new arrivals were little more than yachts and very extreme designs were introduced. Built in 1869, the *Cutty Sark* was a survivor of this era, but in many ways she was not a typical tea clipper. She had a slightly heavier look to her stern, higher bulwarks and slightly rough, unfinished sides, which lacked the perfect yacht-like sheen of the normal tea clipper. She also lacked the 'ghosting' qualities of a typical China clipper and was far more at home tearing through the Roaring Forties before a gale than floating before a fickle breeze.

End of an era

The year of the *Cutty Sark*'s launch, 1869, also marked the end of an era. It was the year that De Lesseps opened the Suez Canal. In a stroke the clippers were rendered redundant, as a steamship could have her cargo home in 50 days or less. Although they raced desperately on, competition slowly fizzled out. The *Cutty Sark* and the *Thermopylae* retreated to the Australian wool

The *Flying Cloud* at the peak of her powers. This gallant vessel survived until 1874. Reduced to a lumber trader, she went ashore off New Brunswick and her hull was burnt for its scrap metal.

trade where they continued to race for many years – and with unparalleled success – against larger, less extreme iron clippers. The zenith of British clippers had passed and, although they raced on, their star was fading.

After 1880, commercial sailing ships became slaves to ever decreasing freights. Iron and steel took over from wood and every year the fleet of tall ships diminished in number, the last being snuffed out by the Second World War. Even as the last of the windjammers battled on, sailors mourned the loss of the true clipper ships. Never again would they experience the unparalleled thrill of feeling a large ship tremble like a leaf as she raced down tumbling seas, pushed to her very limit. The skills required to keep one of these big ships moving are also long forgotten. Yet we can still remember and celebrate the ships and some of the characters whose remarkable seamanship made the passages of these beautiful clippers news the world over.

This book focuses on the captains who commanded these ships, all in their own way a cut above the average. Many were larger-than-life figures, often feared and generally flawed. Yet it took a very special and determined sort of character to get the best out of a clipper ship and there is no doubt that many of these captains were truly exceptional. Often, they earned command at a very young age, having distinguished themselves well beyond a normal skipper. Without a good captain, even the fastest ship was useless and without these determined commanders the clippers would have been nothing.

The following chapters are a selection of stories told in fo'c'sles long after the ships and captains had gone. In the twilight of commercial sail, mariners kept their memory alive, spinning out their yarns in the off watches. Sitting by the binnacle on a tropical night or hiding in the fo'c'sle on a dark day off Cape Horn, these stories were told, embroidered and then retold. This book is an attempt to preserve some of them, for they deserve to be remembered. All of them are true.

CHAPTER TWO

A HELL SHIP VOYAGE WITH 'BULLY' WATERMAN

New York 1851. A young skipper swaggers down South Street like he owns the place. His name is Robert Waterman and his fame is such that he is known across the city. Waterman pauses outside the offices of ship owners NL&G Griswold before heading up the marble staircase of their opulent office. He is about to make the worst decision of his life, one that will leave his reputation in tatters and end with him being hunted by the law and an angry lynch mob.

This tale has its roots in the Californian gold rush. Ever since the discovery of Californian gold in 1849, the country had been in the grip of a fever, as prospectors from all walks of life raced to the gold fields, chasing the American dream. Gold fever also heralded the most exciting era of shipbuilding the US had ever witnessed. Clipper ships formed a vital supply line to the gold fields and, from 1849 until the end of the rush in 1854, each successive year saw taller, sharper, faster vessels leaving the east coast shipyards. These beautiful clippers were queens of the seas; in heavy weather no ship could touch them and their arrival in port was always news. Names like the *Flying Cloud*, the *Romance of the Seas* and the *Great Republic* captured the bullish optimism of young America at its most confident, and these lordly vessels with their snowy white canvas and rakish beauty were a powerful symbol of the country's newfound belief.

Captain Waterman was arguably the most talented skipper of the American clipper ship era. He had risen to his first command at the unusually young age of 28, several years before the discovery of gold in California. An exacting man, he drove himself hard, and his crew even harder, to get his ship moving. He was also not afraid to use force. A few trips in the transatlantic trade had earned him the nickname 'Bully' Waterman.

Robert Waterman, young captain and doyen of New York society.

In 1842 he was given command of an old cotton packet, the *Natchez*, which was put into the burgeoning China trade. The *Natchez* had been built with a flat bottom to help her get over the New Orleans bar and, while this had helped in her cotton days, it meant she was known in shipping circles as a heavy sluggard with poor sailing qualities. Yet Waterman's hard driving and uncanny knack of finding a breeze turned her into the fastest and most consistent vessel in the trade, her zenith being a record-breaking run from China to New York of 78 days. This was a remarkable performance and Waterman enjoyed plaudits all round. His reward was a new ship, the *Sea Witch*, seen by many as the first true clipper of the era. She was well ahead of her time and the combination of a fast ship with Waterman in command was unbeatable. In 1848 he broke his own China record with a run of 77 days, a passage that has never been bettered.

Fame and fortune
Success turned Waterman into a celebrity in New York society and, when in town, he strutted through the streets clad in a fabulous suit of Chinese silk, every inch the young player. He had his pick of the women, too, and became known as something of a dandy, moving in rarefied circles and attracting admiring looks from society girls. By 1848 Waterman had made his fortune; he was a rich man and his reputation as the clipper captain *par*

Overleaf: **The clippers** *Flying Fish* **and** *Wild Pigeon* **racing around the Horn in 1853. The** *Flying Fish* **made the excellent time of 92 days from New York to San Francisco.**

The *Sea Witch* was one of the first true clippers and under the command of Waterman she set some truly astonishing records in the China tea trade.

A view of the Hudson River and New York beyond, seen from Brooklyn circa 1820.

The *Challenge* on the stocks at William Webb's yard.

Below and opposite bottom: Two views of Boston Harbour during the clipper era.

excellence was unsurpassed. He married Cordelia, one of the beautiful society girls, and retired to a peaceful existence in California, a million miles from both the glamorous New York life and his brutal sailing days.

It seemed like the end of a chapter for the greatest captain of a generation. Waterman held the belief that the day of the sailing ship was nearly over and that the glamour and celebrity attached to the clippers was on the wane. To him, future success seemed to lie away from the waves.

However, the 1849 gold rush changed all that and the scramble to get to San Francisco thrust clipper ships back into the spotlight. Suddenly the deeds of some of Waterman's contemporary and, to his mind, lesser skippers were headline news. Fraser, his mate, had taken over command of the *Sea Witch* and was basking in the limelight after a record passage out to the gold fields. New ships were being launched and records Waterman had set in the *Sea Witch* were shattered.

Back in New York on a family visit, Waterman started to feel a little wistful for the glamour and celebrity he had left behind when he settled down with Cordelia. He was still a young man and still vain. As he walked along South Street admiring some of the big new clippers, he couldn't help but

wonder if he had one final glorious passage left in him. Later that day he strolled along the waterfront to William Webb's shipyard.

The yard was a hive of activity, and shipwrights swarmed over the shapely frames of three clippers on the stocks. Waterman was deeply impressed with the largest one, the *Challenge*, which was being built for NL&G Griswold. He decided to head for their office and make enquiries.

A challenge for the *Challenge*

The merchants NL&G Griswold were canny operators and their company had gained the nickname 'No Loss and Great Gain Griswold'. They were delighted to meet Waterman; his celebrity lived on in shipping circles and they had no trouble luring him back into this new and exciting world. They explained that the *Challenge* was intended to eclipse all that had gone before her. At 230 ft long, she was the biggest, sharpest lined and most heavily sparred vessel ever built and the Griswolds spared no effort in persuading Captain Waterman to command her.

As an added inducement, they offered him a $10,000 bonus if he made the run to San Francisco in under 90 days. For a man of Waterman's talents, it was an achievable challenge and too much for his

The *Flying Cloud* loading at New York prior to her record-breaking maiden voyage.

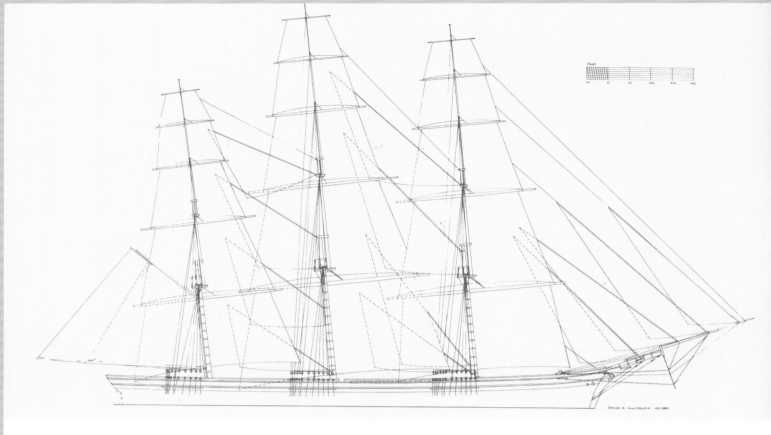

This sail plan of the *Challenge* illustrates the proportions of the massive spars that Waterman insisted she carried.

The *Challenge* at sea. This picture must have been painted later in her life as her sail plan seems much more modest than originally specified. During the fitting out of the clipper, Waterman clashed with her designer, William Webb, who originally specified a more manageable sail plan. Her rig was therefore drastically cut down in later years.

A dramatic painting of a clipper ship passing Minot's Light, off the Massachusetts coast.

Another fast clipper ship was the *Golden State*, built in 1852. Here she is seen leaving New York Harbour.

competitive nature to ignore. Lubricated by several drinks from the Griswolds' well-stocked cabinet and glowing with dreams of glory, he signed on as captain. His fate was sealed.

The Griswolds hadn't exaggerated when they had described the *Challenge*. She truly was a remarkable vessel, built to compete with the Boston clippers of Donald McKay, which were cutting a dash at the time. McKay had just completed his masterpiece, the *Flying Cloud*, which was due to leave New York a matter of weeks before the *Challenge*. The rivalry between the two vessels was clear to all and deepened by the competition between these two great shipbuilding cities.

There was a real fear in New York that the Boston yards of McKay and Pook were getting ahead. McKay's *Staghound* had been an extremely innovative ship and the quickest yet to be launched. Now came the *Flying Cloud*, bigger and potentially even faster. The sailing community of New York looked to the *Challenge* to restore its reputation as America's leading shipbuilding city.

Waterman must have taken a look over the *Flying Cloud* as she loaded up on South Street. He would doubtless have admired her clean lines and powerful aspect. The *Flying Cloud* was commanded by Josiah Creesy, who knew Waterman well, even if Waterman didn't remember him. He, too, had been in the China trade and had marvelled at the

remarkable passages Waterman had managed to make. He had driven his own ship as hard as he dared; yet, year after year, Waterman had eclipsed him. Now, with a new ship, Creesy had a chance to show the world what he was capable of achieving. He sailed from New York on 2 June and, a little under three months later, the *Flying Cloud* smashed all records with a run of 89 days to San Francisco.

The *Challenge* had to wait a little longer. Her fitting out was a fraught affair, as Waterman personally supervised her rigging and was dissatisfied with her sail plan, insisting it was too small for his purposes. William Webb, her designer, must have been severely tempted to tell the arrogant skipper to mind his own business. Instead, he held his tongue and extended her already powerful sail plan to extreme proportions.

The *Challenge* was going to be a real handful with this big rig, but Waterman was confident he could whip any crew into shape. On the *Sea Witch* he had been famed for his tough driving style. One story told about him was that on departure, he would order a bucket of seawater to be pulled aboard to 'wash off his shore face'. Henceforth, his shore manners, which so impressed New York society, were gone and Bully Waterman, terror of crews the world over, returned.

Rotten crew

Delays in finding crew meant that the *Challenge* didn't get away until 13 July. Whether Waterman was mindful of the evil omen of sailing on the 13th is unclear, but he ran straight into trouble. All summer, ships had been clearing out of New York headed for the gold fields and by July there was a serious shortage of good-quality sailors. In those days crews were generally secured by means of 'crimps', who drugged potential crew members on the eve of a voyage and smuggled them aboard. The first thing a 'shanghaied' sailor knew about it was waking up with a sore head as the ship slipped out of port.

By the time the *Challenge* was anchored off Sandy Hook preparing to sail, Waterman knew that he had a thoroughly rotten crew made up of

REGULAR LINE
OF CLIPPER SHIPS
FOR SAN FRANCISCO.
ELEGANT CALIFORNIA CLIPPER SHIP!!
Stands Strictly A 1, Extra.

The Magnificent A 1, EXTREME Clipper Ship
SEMIRAMIS
GERRISH, Commander,
Is now rapidly loading at Pier 11, East River.

The particular attention of every California Shipper is respectfully directed to the SEMIRAMIS. She is a Sister Ship of the "YO SEMITE," and was constructed under the personal supervision of CAPT. JOHN S. PRAY; and no expense has been spared to make her one of the FINEST CLIPPERS EVER BUILT IN THE UNITED STATES.

Having 1000 TONS OF GOVERNMENT FREIGHT engaged, her capacity for General Cargo is very small.

A Quick Passage and Perfect Delivery of Cargo are certain.

CORNELIUS COMSTOCK & CO.,
106 WALL STREET.
Consignee at San Francisco, Mr. ALBERT DIBBLEE.

N. B.—Shippers will please observe that all vessels loaded in this Line are popular California Clippers, and always have very quick dispatch in loading.

Sailing ship cards were common in the US and were handed out to advertise the departure of a vessel to shippers.

The *Challenge* at sea.

landlubbers and jailbirds, many suffering from a range of unsavoury diseases. To make matters worse, Waterman chose this moment to argue with his mate, who was ultimately responsible for recruiting this miserable bunch. Firing him on the spot, the mate was sent ashore, while the captain fumed aboard. Waterman must have been sorely tempted to demand a fresh crew, but time was pressing and he had to get to San Francisco by 11 October to pick up the $10,000 prize money.

He later conceded that at this point he had considered turning back, but pride and vanity were too great and pushed him onward to disaster. As Waterman paced the poop, pondering his ill fortune, a longboat pulled alongside carrying a man by the name of Jim Douglass. 'Black Douglass' had served his time on the transatlantic packet run and had earned a reputation as a veritable fiend for whipping the surly Scouse 'packet rats' into shape. He pulled alongside the *Challenge* with the express intention of cutting and running from a vengeful crew that he had knocked about on the passage from Liverpool. Waterman hired him there and then.

Shortly afterwards, the *Challenge* made sail and slipped away from New York. Waterman summoned all hands and made the usual speech about fair treatment, while the mate sneaked forward and turned over their belongings for weapons. This was a sensible precaution, as mutinies and violence were not uncommon. Indeed, the *Flying Cloud*, racing out ahead of them on her way into the history books, had to quell a mutiny during the voyage after a couple of crew members schemed to make the ship divert to Rio by drilling a sizeable hole in her hull. Their bizarre and fool-headed scheme was, however, uncovered and the McKay clipper raced on.

Aboard the *Challenge*, both captain and mate were soon exasperated by the incompetence of their crew; out of a complement of 56, only six could helm and many couldn't speak English. Bearing in mind that the *Challenge* was a finely tuned racing machine, requiring finesse to handle, this was disastrous. Douglass had never been afraid to dole out a little 'belaying pin soup' on truculent crew members, whereby dallying crew were liable to receive a sharp blow to the back of the head with a belaying pin or truncheon. This particular bunch of malingerers needed all the encouragement they could get to climb up the *Challenge*'s towering spars.

An action shot of the barque *Olivebank* leaning into a strong breeze. This photograph gives an excellent impression of the sometimes alarming angle which a tall ship heeled over to and also how vital it was for crew to hang on tight in heavy weather.

In the stormy conditions encountered off the Horn, sailors would often have to wade through icy water to handle the ship.

This picture, taken from the rigging of a tall ship, shows very clearly how terrifying the swaying yards of a clipper could be in a storm.

Overleaf: The *Flying Cloud* battling her way through the Cape Horn seas on her way to San Francisco.

Crew at work bending a topsail and illustrating how tenuous your position was when working high up aloft.

The mood of the officers was not helped by the ship's slow progress down the North Atlantic; the *Challenge* seemed dogged by light winds and progress was painful. By the time the doldrums around the equator had been reached, the ship was a truly oppressive place to be and the crew sweltered and squabbled through the tropics, their own smouldering anger stoked by the mate's red hot fury.

Trouble broke out after allegations of thieving. Douglass opted to turn out the crew's belongings on deck – with a little encouragement from his trusty truncheon. Conflict came from an unusual source. There were four decent sailors on board who spoke English and were generally favoured by the mates. Unfortunately, one of these had a marlinspike in his sea chest and Douglass pounced on it, berating the man for thieving. It was too much for the wrongly accused seaman, who flew on the

mate in an absolute fury, pinning him to the ground. The rest of the crew, seizing their opportunity to exact revenge on their hated oppressor, rushed the pair and piled on the mate as he lay on the floor. Douglass was stabbed in the leg at this point, and there is little doubt that he would have been killed if Waterman hadn't been alerted by a passenger.

At the time, the captain had been taking sights on the poop, and he reacted quickly, wading in and smashing the mate's assailants with his sextant. The men hesitated and were overpowered. The man who had punched Douglass was sought out, but he had disappeared and it was asserted that he had jumped overboard in terror.

From then on, the *Challenge* turned into a veritable hell ship as Douglass sought revenge for what he and Waterman saw as mutiny. The key troublemakers were severely flogged by Douglass,

The *Flying Cloud* making her final approach to the Golden Gate in 1851. During the passage she was partially dismasted twice and two of her crew drilled a hole in the hull in a desperate attempt to scare her captain into stopping in Rio.

Opposite top: A clipper approaching the end of its voyage. No matter how harmonious a ship was, it was always a relief to reach your final destination. In the case of the *Challenge*, all aboard must have been eager to finally make San Francisco.

Opposite bottom: The *Challenge* arrived in San Francisco after a 108-day passage, but all was not well aboard.

who later conceded that he couldn't remember how many lashes he had doled out. For the first time on an already unpleasant trip, the *Challenge*'s decks ran red with blood.

Crisis at Cape Horn

The stunned crew grew surlier and less inclined to work, not helped by the fact that all this time the *Challenge* was working her way toward the bleak, icy waters of Cape Horn. Beating into the Roaring Forties, as these wild waters are known, is no place for amateurs; and there is little doubt that these men were almost useless. Many did not have shoes so walking the decks, awash with icy water and slush, would have been agony. Some simply retired to their bunks and had to be forcibly put to work.

The *Challenge* was rounding Cape Horn at the very height of the southern winter, with gates blowing savagely from the west for days on end. Hurricane force winds lashed the vessel to the point where her lengthy yardarms dipped their tips in the icy grey water. Day after day, giant waves thundered all around the clipper, threatening to inundate and overwhelm her slender form. Up above, the rigging let out a magnificent and utterly terrifying roar that can only ever be heard on a tall ship in a very heavy storm.

Waterman was a consummate seaman, yet even he was struggling to get through this icy torment and almost went down to the Antarctic Circle in the hope of gaining a bit of westing to weather the dreaded cape and begin the run up to the warmer climes of the Pacific. It was down in this hell on earth that the worst atrocities were committed against the crew. First, there was a demoralising accident as the second mate's watch tried to furl the *Challenge*'s massive topsail. Several crew members reluctantly climbed to the maintop, but there they remained, shivering and terrified. Fear had paralysed them and they refused to climb out on to the massive yard.

The second mate, a man by the name of Coghill, ascended the mast. Cursing and snarling, he had to literally kick his men out onto the wildly swaying yard to get them to bring the sail in. Down on deck, Douglass, impatient at the delay, eased the braces to spill the wind, yelling at Coghill to get his 'sons of bitches' to get hold of the flogging sail. Perhaps the mate's agitation was why the braces were released too rapidly, allowing the mighty topsail yard to swing free and then pull taut with a sickening twang that catapulted four men off and sent them, plummeting into the icy sea, a

Another William Webb clipper, the *Young America*, lying alongside the wharf at San Francisco.

maelstrom of giant breaking waves. They were immediately lost and nothing could be done. There were mutterings among the crew that Douglass had done it deliberately.

This was highly doubtful, but Douglass was unquestionably getting out of control. He was in acute pain from his own leg wound and his inept crew seemed to whip him into a sadistic rage. One of the most notorious malingerers was hurled into the freezing scuppers after refusing to go up the rigging and then lashed to the rail for an hour in the midst of a blizzard. Shortly afterwards, he died. Another crew member, a particularly incompetent elderly Italian known as PawPaw, also refused duty. When confronted by the mate, he gestured to his bare feet, completely swollen and unusable due to frostbite. Douglass bellowed at him to get moving, but PawPaw simply gabbled in Italian and the mate handed him such a beating that he died a few hours later.

In the midst of all this, Douglass determined to find the seaman who had stabbed him in the leg several weeks before. The crew had sworn that he had jumped overboard in terror, but Douglass didn't believe them and opted to make a thorough search of the fo'c'sle. Eventually the man was found hidden inside the frame of one of the bunks. Douglass waited for the guilty man to extricate himself from his hiding place and aimed a blow of his truncheon at his head. The man raised his arm to shield himself and the impact of the blow broke it in two places. He was dragged whimpering down below and clapped in irons for the rest of the voyage.

In all, nine crew members died on the passage, some from illness, some in accidents, others from brutal treatment. It was an ugly statistic, one that Waterman must have been pondering as the *Challenge* raced up the Pacific before the trade winds. By now he must have realised that he wasn't going to make his 90-day target and this can't have helped his mood. In fairness, his chances had always been slim as he sailed at an unfavourable time of year with light summer winds in the northern hemisphere, followed by brutal winter storms off Cape Horn.

In the better sailing conditions of the Pacific, Waterman became increasingly annoyed with the incompetence of his helmsmen and made a habit of lingering behind them with his truncheon in hand. If they deviated too far from their course, they could expect a sharp blow to the head. The whole ship simmered with discontent, but with San Francisco and the gold fields within striking distance, an uneasy truce prevailed.

In the end, the *Challenge* sailed through the Golden Gate 108 days out. It was a good passage and she had beaten her nearest rival by two weeks. In fact, no ship ever bettered this time sailing at such an unfavourable time of year. Given his crew and the trouble aboard, it was actually a remarkable achievement. Yet it was utterly overshadowed by the *Flying Cloud*'s 89 days, celebrated the world over. Besides, the scandal brewing would make passage times irrelevant.

The reckoning in San Francisco

The clipper swung to her anchor in San Francisco Bay, awaiting a berth alongside the wharves. While Waterman and Douglass remained aboard, the surviving crew rapidly decamped to the bars of San Francisco, where they told, and no doubt embroidered, their tales of brutality. Stories of Waterman and his mate throwing sailors over the side still alive abounded and rumours of unimaginable cruelty spread across the city like wildfire.

San Francisco during the heady days of the gold rush was a city growing uncontrollably as thousands of prospectors descended upon it to seek their fortune. The waterfront was littered with hundreds of ships that had sailed in and then been abandoned as crew and officers alike cut and ran for the gold fields, leaving their vessels to rot.

Many prospectors set up home in makeshift tents on the hillsides of the city and every few weeks fire would sweep through these shanty towns, decimating the dwellings and generally causing panic. The authorities were always struggling to keep up with policing the city as it expanded and there was a genuine sense of lawlessness. Among

Overleaf: **A view of San Francisco as it was in the early days of the gold rush. Although the town is still a tiny, ramshackle affair, the harbour is already crowded with ships, many abandoned and left to rot.**

STARKEY, JANION & CO.

the streets, crammed with gambling houses, drinking dens and brothels, vigilantes took the law into their own hands.

As tales of the *Challenge* spread around town, hysteria started to set in, not helped by an article in the *California Courier* that read: 'The ship *Challenge* has arrived and Capt Waterman, her commander has also – but where are nine of her crew? And where is he and his guilty mate? The accounts given of Waterman towards his men, if true, make him one of the most inhumane monsters of this age. If they are true, he should be burned alive – he should never leave this city a live man.' The article went on to describe Waterman as a 'beast in human form' and detailed the hair-raising tale of the four men that had been shaken off the mainyard off Cape Horn.

As the ship was towed alongside the wharf at San Francisco, an angry mob had formed with the express intention of executing Waterman and his mate. The pair were in real danger at this moment. Earlier in the year, a mob had taken it upon themselves to dispense justice to a pair of Australians accused of robbery, while in 1856 a 6,000-member vigilante group was assembled after a couple of high-profile shooting incidents. This lynch mob hanged the suspects without trial. Waterman realised the best thing was to show no fear and, with customary bravado, he marched ashore, overawing the mob leaders and heading to his agent's offices.

While the mob awaited Douglass, it became more vociferous and the mate realised that caution might well be the better part of valour. As the ship was being unloaded, he arranged to slip over the side into a rowing boat, which would enable him to enter the city at a more secluded place. Unfortunately, as the rowing boat slid away, the mob spotted him and immediately gave chase. Spurred on by pure fear, Douglass headed into the eerie maze of rotting ships in the harbour, disappearing into the dark, dripping recesses of this nightmarish labyrinth, and rowed for dear life.

Three different views of San Francisco in the heady days of the gold rush. Many ships were abandoned as crews cut and ran to the gold fields up country. Some ships sank at their anchors, while others were converted into ramshackle makeshift quays, jetties and even bars and warehouses.

Once Waterman departed the *Challenge*, she sailed on, making a passage to England loaded with tea. Here, she is seen arriving off the South Coast.

Sweating profusely both with exertion and pure fear, Douglass played a dangerous game of hide and seek with his pursuers. In the dark gloom between narrowly packed ships, all would be silent. Momentarily he would burst back out into the burning bright sunlight to hear the roars of the chasing pack. Sometimes he would glance back and fear would spur him to new exertions and he leant heavily into his oars, hurling the skiff forward with each powerful stroke. He finally succeeded in losing the mob and made for the city, ramming the boat up a beach and abandoning it there. He leapt ashore and was lost within the anonymity of San Francisco's ramshackle streets. He didn't stop moving either, literally running for the Californian hills.

In the meantime, the dissatisfied mob turned its attention back to Waterman. He was in NL&G Griswold's San Francisco office when the mob descended, baying for blood. In the ensuing melee, he was compelled to escape via the roof and a drainpipe, leaving the incensed crowd on the verge of a full-blown riot. As the shadows lengthened on a very long day for Waterman, he slipped out of town. Douglass, meanwhile, was caught hiding in a hay cart several miles away. On being arrested he said: 'Well, gentlemen, if you want to hang me, here's a pretty tree, do it like men.'

Waterman and Douglass, along with the second mate Coghill, were brought to trial, but their assertion of mutiny put them on strong ground and Waterman was ultimately praised for his handling of a tricky ship with a weak crew. Douglass escaped with a light censure and was free to carry on tormenting crews like the bully he would always be.

Abandoned ships left to rot along the wharves of San Francisco. Some were still in use, others were eventually turned into wharves in their own right. The maze of ships formed ideal cover for the fleeing Douglass.

The aftermath

As for Waterman, the *Challenge* cured him of the sea once and for all and he retired to his ranch in California. He took to religion and is reputed to have worked as a missionary in San Francisco, boarding ships and spreading the word of God. The story goes that on one of these soul-saving missions he was recognised by one of his previous crew and unceremoniously slung over the side. He recovered from this dunking and in later years was regarded as a pillar of the community, establishing the settlements of Cordelia and Fairfield in California.

William Webb, who had designed the *Challenge* and held such high hopes for her, was disappointed with her performance, but learnt from her design. He proceeded to turn out some of the finest vessels in the Californian trade, including the *Comet*, the *Swordfish* and the *Young America*, which all succeeded in cementing his reputation as one of the foremost designers of the clipper ship era.

McKay's *Flying Cloud*, meanwhile, actually managed to repeat her 89-day run to San Francisco a couple of years later. It was a passage that was only once equalled again and never beaten.

And what of the *Challenge*? After this unfortunate start in life, she enjoyed very little luck and was forever labelled a 'hell ship'. She did, however, outlast many of her peers, eventually running aground and sinking off the French coast in 1877. Her disastrous maiden voyage left behind a legacy of brutality and violence that gradually became a myth told in hushed tones in wharfside bars and fo'c'sles around the world.

CHAPTER THREE

MARCO POLO
THE FASTEST SHIP IN THE WORLD

In every life there are highs and lows. For some this rise and fall of fortune is little more than a gentle undulation, the moderate groundswell of our life that keeps things moving along. Yet there are others for whom a groundswell is not enough and who push on recklessly, often racing headlong into catastrophe in search of that thrill of risk that confirms they are truly alive. James Nichol Forbes, the master of the *Marco Polo*, *Lightning* and *Schomberg*, was one such character. He reached the peak of his profession and then threw himself, almost wilfully, into a tidal wave of catastrophe.

James Forbes had left Liverpool in 1855 at his peak: newly married, wealthy and in command of the *Schomberg*, the largest and finest sailing ship ever built in Britain to date. He was commodore of the famous Black Ball Line of passenger ships and one of the most respected captains in the world. A little more than six months later, on the morning of 4 January 1856, all of his fame and achievements had turned to dust. The *Schomberg* had just been wrecked off the Melbourne coast and even as Forbes sat in one of the town's better

appointed hotels awaiting orders from the owner, his former passengers were holding a meeting with the express intention of destroying the reputation of their famous captain.

The meeting was held in the Melbourne Mechanics Institution and the first resolution was to prove that 'the conduct of the Captain of the *Schomberg* was ungentlemanly, discourteous, tyrannical and grossly immoral'. It was a well-attended and boisterous affair. As the beleaguered Forbes paced his hotel room pondering his change

Melbourne in 1854.

An artist's impression of Captain James Forbes.

of fortune, the meeting was agog with titillating tales of his lack of moral fibre.

'The captain entertained two "lady" passengers in the second cabin,' piped up one good Victorian. 'These females were kept out of their cabins by the captain and his officers until very unseasonable hours. One was kept up until one in the morning, while the other preferred daylight for she returned to her cabin at four in the morning and then only in her nightdress!'

This final statement was greeted with cheers of agreement and delight. The knives were out, and the meeting ended in uproarious fashion, with Forbes being denounced again and again. Later that day, when Forbes left his hotel, he was greeted by titters and guffaws at every turn.

How different things had been the previous year when he had arrived in this town aboard the *Lightning*, respected as the greatest captain to have ever set foot on Australian soil. One stranding later and his life had utterly capsized.

A stranding with a twist
As a matter of fact, James Forbes' meteoric career was bookended by two strandings. The second, discussed with so much relish in Melbourne, was

50

Above: The *Lightning*, probably the fastest vessel Forbes ever commanded.

Right: A wooden schooner on the stocks at a US shipyard.

Overleaf: The *Marco Polo* at sea.

seared onto the captain's memory forever, but for the first he was several thousand miles away. Yet that first stranding was also to have a profound effect on his career. Back in 1850, Canadian shipbuilder James Smith had decided to build a new vessel with the intention of sailing her to Liverpool and selling her. All through the autumn and winter, workmen had been frenziedly shaping and sawing at Smith's yard at Courtenay Bay on the outskirts of St John, New Brunswick. By spring 1851 the 185 ft clipper *Marco Polo* lay poised to make the brief transition from land to sea.

As the winter progressed the residents of Courtenay Bay had watched and listened as the ship grew a shadow. The whining of the saw, swish of the axe and thud of the adze had been a symphony that had accompanied her construction. The streets around the yard were full of the sweet smell of sawdust as her ribs slowly swayed, one by one, up into place, casting thin shadows in the

The port of Liverpool in the 1850s was a thriving hub of emigrant ships.

low winter sunlight. Then had come the hiss of the steambox and the pounding of treenails as her great frame was planked. She was evidently a very large ship, her great hull now blotting out the light of the sun, and as the caulker's mallet rang out through town, locals gathered to assess the new vessel.

She didn't look much like a clipper at all and many proclaimed they thought her damn ugly. At the time she was described as 'a great brick of a boat, with a bow like a savage bulldog'. With her painted ports and angular stern she looked more like a warship than the sylph-like vessels being launched in the US and UK, yet she was as sharp as a wedge below the waterline and very deep for her length. Many in the know said she would travel fast if she was pushed hard enough.

Now she was poised to leave, carrying the hopes of the town with her to places they had never seen. All eyes focused on the foreman and his men as their mallets swung away to remove the chocks and she started to slide down the ways. Things were going smoothly. The first challenge of getting the boat moving was achieved. The next was stopping her, and it was at this point that things started to go wrong. The check wires that the yard used to slow the boat down were meant to come into play and, as the weight of the ship started to load them up, there was an almighty explosion. As overloaded hemp

and chain parted, the *Marco Polo* careered across the bay out of control, colliding stern first on a mud bank, and then sheering around horribly in the tide, injuring several people aboard when chains, barrels and other debris went by the board.

Disaster! The town looked on, dumbstruck with horror, then seemed to move bodily towards the water. Men swarmed into boats in an endeavour to free her. Yet for all the prompt action, it took five days to free the stranded vessel. Worse was to come: as she lay those five days at the mercy of the tide, it became evident that her shapely hull was twisting and sagging under the pressure of her unnatural position and the power of the tide dragging her to and fro. Her owner and builder wrung his hands watching her lie there stricken and breathed a sigh of relief when she was finally freed. It was an evil omen, and many old salts in the town shook their heads when they looked across at her fitting out. 'She'll never sail,' they said, eyeing her slightly wonky lines with relish.

They were wrong. Leaving St John loaded with lumber for Liverpool, she made the trip in the remarkably swift time of 15 days. Her powerful lines and weighty build ensured that she could be driven very hard in heavy weather, but her captain proclaimed that there was something else about the boat, some miracle of her design and construction that kept her flying when others slowed. Many argued that the twist in her hull was the making of the vessel.

Under new ownership

The *Marco Polo*'s 15-day passage went largely unnoticed and her owner had to wait for her second trip to Liverpool, this time from the port of Mobile, Alabama, before he found a buyer for his creation. Smith travelled with the ship and, arriving in Liverpool, he hoisted a broom to the top of her mainmast. This was the sign that a ship was for sale and this time there was no trouble finding a buyer. Shipping was booming, and whispers of the discovery of gold in Australia were already filtering into the taverns of Liverpool and London. By 1852 these rumours had grown to hysteria and men and women from all walks of life were clamouring to head for the gold fields of New South Wales. Poised to exploit this was James Baines, a Liverpool merchant whose Black Ball Line of packets had flourished on the Atlantic run. Baines saw that the time was right to expand and sought out cheap ships to put on the Australia run. The *Marco Polo* fitted the bill perfectly.

Baines had gambled on an unusual new ship and rolled the dice again with the appointment of her new skipper, James Forbes. A lean, energetic Scotsman of 32, Forbes was unusually young to be captain of a large passenger vessel. He had risen to the attention of Baines after managing to drive one of his most truculent ships out to Argentina and back in excellent time. Now he faced a fresh challenge, for the Australian trip was a long, hard slog. The beat out of the English Channel and across Biscay was tough enough, but from the Cape of Good Hope to Australia one could expect a fairly hair-raising trip across the Roaring Forties.

In those days, emigrant ships were crammed with passengers, with death and disease a constant menace. The shorter the passage the better, and Baines knew it was vital to establish a reputation for a fast service. In Forbes he saw a young man with grit and determination, a man young enough and with enough fire in the belly to take the strain of driving a ship on for 80 days and more at a time.

Up through the hawse-pipe

James Forbes was certainly a driven man. It took an exceptional sailor to gain command at such

The gold fields of Ballarat, Australia, were a magnet for adventurers and dreamers throughout the world.

Emigrants embarking aboard a departing ship. On her first voyage, the *Marco Polo* was badly overloaded, and many passengers perished.

The discomfort aboard the *Marco Polo* in foul weather is clearly conveyed in this depiction of life aboard an emigrant ship.

a young age and he had done it the hard way. 'Coming up through the hawse-pipe' was the expression for a skipper who had started out as cabin boy and worked his way up. Forbes had left his native town of Aberdeen at the age of 18 and headed to Liverpool, the epicentre of the shipping world. By his mid-twenties he had already gained a command. Unlike many of the somewhat stoical skippers of the clipper ship era, Forbes was a brash character, larger than life and a natural showman. He craved fame and recognition and had already witnessed how Captain 'Bully' Waterman in the US had gained celebrity through his feats of sailing; Forbes wanted some of that for himself.

Like Waterman, he rapidly gained the nickname 'Bully' and, just like his namesake, he pushed his crew as hard as he pushed his boat. To make a passage was everything and everyone else could go to hell as far as he was concerned. One thing that Forbes lacked was any kind of finesse when it came to dealing with people. He was working class, foul-mouthed and unashamed of it. In many ways, these attributes were to be his undoing.

First came success and Forbes had plenty of it. The *Marco Polo* left Liverpool for Melbourne on 4 July 1852, loaded with 932 emigrants from all walks of life. Some were gentlemen prospectors, to whom the thrill of gold was simply too great to resist, but the larger proportion were much poorer and far more desperate. In the cramped conditions in steerage class the best hope was to get there as quickly as possible. Prior to this voyage, Bully Forbes had certainly given many of them reason to be hopeful by proclaiming that the ship would be back in Liverpool within six months. Given that many ships took that length of time to get out to Melbourne, many saw this as little more than an idle boast and paid scant attention. There is little doubt that James Baines, the owner, smiled somewhat indulgently at his fiery skipper's bold proclamation and simply hoped he'd get there in under 100 days – anything under this mark was a good passage by the standard of the day.

The months passed by and Baines awaited news of the arrival of his new vessel. By Christmas he was getting twitchy. Surely she should have arrived out by now? Still, no news of his vessel had been brought home and the wait continued. All this time

Baines wryly pondered on the preposterousness of Forbes' six-month round trip claim. On Boxing Day he received a nasty jolt. He was accosted in the street by a messenger boy informing him that the *Marco Polo* had returned.

'Nonsense, boy, she hasn't even arrived in Melbourne yet,' was his startled answer and he hurried down to the docks, fearing the worst. Surely some mistake? Had she met with some misfortune forcing her to turn back? Turning a corner, Baines espied her hauling into Salthouse Dock. Between her fore and mainmast she flew a banner roughly daubed by a seaman's hand bearing the legend: 'The fastest ship in the world.' The *Marco Polo* had made it around the world in five months and 21 days – far quicker than any before her.

Troubles on the record passage

The trip had been a tough one, and lurid rumours abounded about Forbes' desperate cracking on to make the passage. Seamen leaving the boat told tales of wild nights when the *Marco Polo* had shivered to her very seams and how the captain had threatened them with a pistol to prevent them from shortening sail. There were stories of confrontation with the passengers and of how an outbreak of smallpox had left 35 dead on the outward passage.

It was probably on this passage that the 'Hell or Melbourne' incident occurred. The story goes that one dark night the *Marco Polo* was staggering along under far too much sail. Down below the passengers were in acute discomfort as the boat lurched and groaned. In the dark 'tween decks there would be the occasional almighty thump as the vessel pounded into a heavy sea. All would cower for fear that either the masts had finally come loose or that she had given up and was about to sink. Many of the passengers were seasick in these miserable conditions and gathered in little knots to discuss their miserable lot. The general conclusion was that it was all the captain's fault.

Overleaf: **The *Marco Polo* on her maiden voyage under the Black Ball Line. The Black Ball flag flies from her mainmast. This painting gives a good impression of how heavy and ungainly the *Marco Polo* looked compared to other clippers.**

Even the handiest tall ship was still relatively cumbersome to handle in restricted waters and this meant that making a landfall required extra care. Here, a clipper beats away from a rocky coastline.

Eventually one gentleman decided it was high time to do something about it. Struggling up on to the freezing, spray-lashed deck, he battled his way to the weather rail, where Forbes stood impassively observing the carnage, one arm hooked under the rail to steady himself. Above the roar of the wind in the rigging and between dunkings in the walls of spray that were battering the pair, this gentleman asked Forbes what the devil he thought he was playing at. Forbes replied without hesitation: 'It's a case of Hell or Melbourne, I'm afraid, sir.' And that was that.

The *Marco Polo* made it out to Melbourne in 68 days, beating the steamer *Australia* by a week in the process. The return passage around Cape Horn occupied 76 days and Forbes found that the *Marco Polo*'s deep draught and full lines above the waterline gave her a capacity to fly in the Roaring Forties and Screaming Fifties. She could take all the driving he could muster, yet she was also surprisingly quick in light airs. This combination was her real strength. Then there was also that secret ingredient, the miracle of the ship, wrapped up in that twist in the hull inadvertently added by a friendly sandbank.

Forbes was rightly lauded for his circumnavigation and he was a made man on his return to Liverpool. The most famous captain in Britain, Forbes found that celebrity suited him. He was a born extrovert, very fond of grandiose gestures, and made more than a few wine-infused promises of even greater passages at the many dinners held in his honour. His departure from Liverpool on his second voyage was done in suitably swashbuckling style. Addressing his passengers as they towed out of the Mersey, Forbes proclaimed: 'Ladies and gentlemen, on our last voyage, I astonished the world with the sailing of this ship. This time, I intend to astonish even God almighty!' As Liverpool receded, Forbes knew he had a lot to live up to, but he made it to Melbourne in the good time of 75 days and was back again in Liverpool in under six months.

Commander of the *Lightning*
On his return, Forbes was appointed skipper of Baines' new ship, the *Lightning*. This vessel was 254 ft long, far bigger than the *Marco Polo*. She was built by Donald McKay of Boston, who was already

Hobsons Bay was the entrance to the city of Melbourne from the sea and emigrants would have lined the rail to get their first sight of their new home.

Below: The storm-ravaged coastline of the Kerguelen Islands.

Overleaf: The *Red Jacket* cautiously feeling her way through a huge ice field down in the depths of the Southern Ocean. This was during her race home from Australia with *Lightning* and she very nearly became completely trapped in the ice. Despite escaping, she lost precious time.

Three clippers lie in Hobsons Bay, Melbourne. To the left is the *Kent,* in the centre is the *Lightning* and to the right is the *Shalimar.* All the ships are drying and airing their sails.

famous for the legendary *Flying Cloud*, which had broken the record from New York to San Francisco in 1852. The *Lightning* was, if anything, a more extreme vessel and her waterlines were incredibly sharp and hollow. Above the waterline she was actually very clumsy to look at from some angles. Forbes didn't care too much for looks; all he cared about was the fact that her greater waterline length gave her greater potential for speed.

He was sent over to Boston to collect the new vessel and immediately put her to the test. On the tenth day out, she made 436 nautical miles in 24 hours. It was a phenomenal run. On this day, Forbes noted the following in his log book: 'Carried away fore topsail and lost jib. Hove up the log several times and found the ship going through the water at a rate of 18 to 18 and a half knots. Lee rail underwater and rigging slack.' The *Lightning* arrived in Liverpool in the remarkable time of 13 days, a record at the time and one that won Forbes yet more plaudits.

The clipper loaded for Melbourne and was pitted against the *Red Jacket*, which had also been built in Boston and was being chartered by the White Star Line, a rival Liverpool shipping company. The *Red Jacket* was of similar dimensions to the *Lightning* and had also raced across from the US in 13 days. Many bets were placed on the outcome of this race.

The *Red Jacket* got away first and made it out to Melbourne in 67 days, one day quicker than the *Marco Polo*'s best time. Bully Forbes was considerably less fortunate with his winds. A big vessel like the *Lightning* needed a gale to really get her going, but the weather stayed predominantly fair for the passage and the *Lightning* arrived in Melbourne after a voyage of 77 days. This was still quick, but not quick enough to back up all the big claims that Forbes had made prior to departure in Liverpool.

The passage also featured a terrifying incident off the Kerguelen Islands, deep in the wilderness of the Southern Ocean. The Kerguelens are a desolate group of islands, uninhabited, surrounded by savage rocks and pounded relentlessly by the lonely sea. They acted as a useful signpost for skippers navigating this great empty stretch of water and Forbes no doubt aimed slightly to leeward of them as a means of getting a firm 'fix' of his position.

As night fell on 16 July, he knew he was in the vicinity and the lookout was urged to be extra vigilant on watch. No attempt was made to slow the *Lightning* down. Shortly after 10 pm came the cry of 'land ahead'; the vessel was headed straight for this treacherous group of islands. The helm was put down, but shortly there was another cry of 'land ahead'. The clipper had raced right into the labyrinth of islands and, within minutes, the cry of 'breakers on the lee bow' rang out. They were surrounded.

Many of the sailors perceived that the game was up and set about distributing life jackets. Passengers tumbled out of bed to eye the snow-covered Kerguelens, lashed as they were by brutal breakers. All awaited the final sickening crunch and inevitable freezing death. It never came. By some miracle, Forbes managed to con his ship through the islands on that bleak, dark night. The following day, he boasted to his passengers that it was all intentional, but there were many who shook their heads at his recklessness.

Forbes had 'got away with it', but the slow passage out meant he had it all to do on the return leg. Again, her rival, the *Red Jacket,* got away first and was running well until near Cape Horn when she sailed into a huge field of ice.

At one point it looked as if she was hopelessly embayed, but after many hours of frantically scanning the horizon, the skipper managed to force a way out and, despite the damage, made an excellent passage of 73 days. James Baines must have wondered what his celebrity skipper could do to counter this. Badly beaten on the passage out, he had to make up time on the return. He did just that, reaching Liverpool in the record time of 63 days.

This is a run that was rarely approached again and never bettered by a commercial sailing ship. Forbes was truly on top of his game and the phenomenal run home meant that he had beaten the *Red Jacket* on elapsed time, despite her two very fine runs. James Baines was delighted. Forbes was made commodore of the fleet and given command of an even larger clipper, the *Schomberg*, which had just been built by a British shipbuilder, Alexander Hall of Aberdeen. She was the biggest sailing ship ever built in the UK and great hopes were entertained that she would put the American shipbuilders back in their place.

Forbes' new command *Lightning* was a huge clipper capable of being driven hard in stormy conditions as this painting illustrates.

The *Schomberg* departing Liverpool at the start of her ill-fated voyage. At the time of her launch, she was the largest sailing ship ever built in the UK.

Passengers saying their final goodbyes before departure.

Steerage passengers often had to make their own entertainment aboard.

A JOLLY GAME.

Imitative Innocent : Here's a lark, Jemmy. This here ship's Schomberg, and that there gas pipe's a hice berg. Now you how close I can go without touching.

A satirical cartoon that came out in the wake of the *Schomberg* incident illustrates how notorious Forbes' reckless behaviour had become.

The *Schomberg*'s only voyage

The *Schomberg* left Liverpool after another endless succession of high falutin' claims from her skipper. From her mainmast flew a banner proclaiming 'Melbourne in 60 days'. All were used to Forbes' ambitious claims by now, but there were plenty whom he had upset along the way and who would have relished seeing him fall.

Baines was aware that many of his passengers were less than enamoured with Forbes' rough and ready ways. They didn't sit well with Victorian niceties of etiquette. As the skipper of some of the most prestigious passenger ships of the time, Forbes was unwittingly drawn into a world of forced manners and charm that his simple, tough upbringing hadn't prepared him for. Yet, with every passage a success, Baines was happy to indulge his star skipper. If the money kept rolling in and the records continued to fall, what was there to worry about? Forbes' lack of manners could easily be brushed off as bluff seaman's talk, with angry words forgotten in the afterglow of yet another successful passage.

The voyage of the *Schomberg* was different. For all of Forbes' promises of Melbourne in 60 days, she took roughly that to get to the Cape of Good Hope and she made the Australian coast in 81 days. It wasn't a dreadful passage, but it was not 60 days. Nevertheless, whatever boasts a skipper has made, a bad passage can be forgiven and the vessel was apparently very heavily laden with machinery and out of trim from the start. There is little doubt that she was unlucky with her winds and 81 days was actually a respectable passage.

Forbes' mistake was that he didn't seem to be able to hide his disgust at the slowness of the trip from his passengers. His relationship with some of the more vocal of these declined as the voyage

Icebergs at sea were feared by all, and Forbes' cavalier approach to them was not appreciated.

Cape Otway was a clear signpost on the way to Melbourne. Forbes missed it as the cape was obscured behind the closer Moonlight Head.

The *Schomberg* freshly launched and being fitted out in Aberdeen.

progressed. It didn't help that he overhauled an American ship at such close quarters that the *Schomberg*'s stunsail boom whipped the flags off her stern. This was a very disrespectful, not to mention dangerous, piece of sailing.

Passengers were also terrified by the reckless manner in which Forbes ran the *Schomberg* in towards an iceberg for them to have a closer inspection. 'So close, she must have touched,' one passenger reflected. The old daredevil spirit could not be shaken off. By the 81st day of the voyage the relationship between skipper and passengers had largely broken down. The real clincher was that Forbes and Hardy, the doctor aboard the *Schomberg*, had become rather too friendly with two lady passengers, frequently entertaining them in the officers' cabins. As the ship approached Australia, there were dark mutterings among the passengers, who saw Forbes as crass, uncouth and worse.

Dangerous gamble
On the evening of 25 December the *Schomberg* was jogging along the Australian coast to Melbourne. Forbes retired below to play cards with one of his young female friends and proceeded to lose. On deck, the watchful mate was under orders to call the skipper if the ship needed to be put about. About 10.30 pm, he judged that the ship was closing the land and went below to inform the captain. Unfortunately Forbes was in a temper and insisted on playing one final hand.

Stepping up on deck 20 minutes later, into the heat of the Australian night, Forbes' anger at losing was sharpened by the tension on deck. The wind was light and a tack was required, but Forbes waited. He was annoyed that it appeared he was being dictated to by his officers, so he let the ship ghost on towards land. Another 20 minutes later, with the surf audibly booming on shore, he finally ordered the *Schomberg* to be put about. Forbes had cut it dangerously fine; the old dare that had scared the *Lightning*'s passengers off the Kerguelen Islands still held firm. He would again impress his authority upon passengers and crew through his extraordinary pluck.

A quick tack was absolutely vital, however, since there was also a strong current setting the ship onshore – a factor that Forbes hadn't reckoned on.

Up went the helm, but the heavy, out-of-trim vessel baulked in the light winds. Ghosting up into the wind she stalled horribly and fell away again. Nothing for it but to get her moving and try something else. In the light wind she clearly wouldn't tack, so Forbes opted to wear ship. This meant that instead of putting the bow through the eye of the wind, the ship ran around in a big circle and switched tacks with the wind on the stern. Sea room was needed for this and a frantic look at the chart suggested there might just be enough. Just.

The crew prepared for this manoeuvre and, as the ship wallowed listlessly, there was the dreaded cry of 'breakers ahead' from the lookout. Up ahead the white surf gleamed in the moonlight. The trap was closing in. Land and destruction were beckoning. It was a nightmare. It looked like Forbes, king of storms, was going to lose his ship in about five knots of wind. Down went the helm this time and the *Schomberg* answered it with painful slowness. Minutes passed agonisingly – everything was happening in slow motion. Even now, Forbes must have thought his lucky charm would hold and the next day this would just be another adventure to relate. It seemed as if he was right. The *Schomberg* was clearly going to get past the breakers and away to safe waters.

Forbes suddenly noticed that by now the passengers lined the moonlit deck, a hushed murmur filling the night air. All eyes were on the captain. In the sticky heat of the tense night, the crew strained at the braces, while a cold sweat prickled Forbes' brow. Then, subtly, almost imperceptibly, the *Schomberg* shuddered. Seconds later, there was a resounding thud as she was picked up by the malevolent swell and thrown bodily onto a sand bar that skirted the reef. She was hard aground.

Forbes stood clutching the rail, numb with shock, paralysed with horror. Yet his fiery character could only react angrily to the situation. The game was up, he realised that, and rage swelled up in his heart. The mate approached him tentatively: 'She's hard aground, sir, what next?' 'Let her go to hell, and let me know when she's on the beach,' he shot back furiously in full earshot of the passengers and stormed below.

The subsequent evacuation of the ship seems to have been supervised by the mate without the

Forbes' next command after the *Lightning* was the *Hastings*, a tubby brig not dissimilar to this one.

Opposite: **Not all wrecks were dramatic affairs involving loss of life. Like the *Schomberg*, the wool clipper *Cromdale*, pictured here, came to a very prosaic end. In this case, the clipper rammed the cliffs off the Cornish coast after her captain lost his bearings in fog.**

Overleaf: Lightning **driven before the storm. She was a ship that revelled in running before the heavy winds of the Southern Ocean. Her high sides ensured that passengers remained dry.**

skipper. It was fortunate that they had grounded on such a calm night and in such a hospitable spot. The evacuation of the vessel was therefore soon achieved without a hitch. Forbes' lack of co-operation was not actually unusual and there were many instances where skippers seemed paralysed after a stranding, but his petulant outburst was noted by many. He had always been good for a sound bite – now it proved his undoing.

The *Schomberg* was abandoned only 35 miles from her destination. While she was pounded to bits in the surf, the passengers gathered for their gleeful protest. Many hoped that the official inquiry would see Forbes stripped of his ticket. Ultimately, though, Forbes held the trump card he had so conspicuously lacked the night of the accident: The sand bar the *Schomberg* had grounded on was uncharted and he was promptly cleared of any blame. In many ways, Forbes had got away with it again.

Decline and fall

Yet, following the wreck, Forbes fell into a decline almost as rapid as his meteoric rise. James Baines was not only his boss but also his friend and was still willing to help his wayward skipper. God knows what he made of the lurid stories coming out of Australia, but he had enough faith in Forbes to give him command of the rather down-at-heel *Hastings*. She was a far cry from the *Lightning*, but she was still a command.

However, Forbes' lucky charm had abandoned him and catastrophe now dogged him at every turn. In 1857, he was arrested in Brisbane after being

The *Lightning* picking up a pilot at the end of her second voyage in 1854. She was now commanded by the popular Captain Enright, who was a teetotaller and did not gamble.

accused by a passenger of assault with intent to rape. The charges were later dropped. Next, the *Hastings*, badly strained and patently unseaworthy, was shifted into the guano trade, the lowest of all operations for a sailing ship. Forbes abandoned her off the South African coast in 1859 with seven feet of water in the hold. He had fallen a long way since the wreck of the *Schomberg* and was described latterly as 'a seedy broken down sort of a man, with the forced jocularity of a broken hearted man'. Several more miserable years and long, demoralising spells languishing 'on the beach' in Calcutta and Forbes was almost finished. Every port he went to, he faced the same pitying looks and heard the same murmured stories of his glory days; a repeated blow upon a bruise that was never allowed to heal.

His last passage in 1867 was a poignant one, for he was reunited with the *Marco Polo*. She, too, was a shadow of her former self, stripped of her status as a passenger vessel, her hull sodden and strained by years of hard use. The pair made one final trip across to Mobile, Alabama, to load cotton. Forbes must have been haunted by former glories as he trod the decks of the tatty old vessel. After this, he retired to Liverpool, where he died a pauper in 1874. He did outlive his epoch-making *Lightning*, which burned to the waterline in 1869 and was scuttled in Geelong, Australia.

Yet the battered old *Marco Polo* sailed on, outliving Forbes by many years. Every year she fell further from grace. Eventually she was reduced to life as a timber carrier and washed around the Atlantic, dishevelled and rotten. Holed up in backwaters, sailors would spot the old timer and, eyeing her with sadness, would speak of her glory days, long gone. She eventually found her resting place not far from her home port of St John in New Brunswick, driven up Cavendish Beach on Prince Edward Island. Here, the fastest ship in the world broke up in the surf, her hull forever twisted out of shape by the pounding waves.

The *Lightning* at sea.

Above: Lightning lasted far longer than most of her fellow Black Ball Line ships and was eventually destroyed by fire off Geelong in 1869. This photo was taken as the fore and mainmasts crashed into the sea. Shortly afterwards she was scuttled.

Above: A clipper ship and a steamer at Portland, Victoria, not far from where *Schomberg* was wrecked. Even in the 1850s much of the Australian coast was poorly charted and local knowledge was very important.

Opposite: Two vessels alongside Circular Quay, Sydney. Together with Melbourne, Sydney was the other main arrival port for emigrants.

Below: The *Lightning* arriving in Hobsons Bay, Melbourne. She continued to make fine passages in the Australian trade under the steadier command of Captain Anthony Enright. Nevertheless, she never bettered her performances under Forbes.

CHAPTER FOUR

MARY PATTEN'S BATTLE WITH CAPE HORN

The clipper *Neptune's Car* had been beating into the teeth of the Roaring Forties for several days when the terrifying apparition appeared. At the time the ship was labouring into a particularly savage gale, which had lashed the great grey waters into a fury. As the lookout peered into the brooding nothingness ahead, spray and hailstones pinged against his body like buckshot, making him wince with pain and gasp with shock. The Cape Horn greybeards had made a mockery of his oilskins and he shivered uncontrollably as he stared into the gloom. He barely had the will to continue his vigil, yet fear of icebergs and a sailor's sense of duty kept him squinting out over the savage waters.

Suddenly, emerging out of the smoking remnants of a squall, he perceived the ghostly outline of a ship. 'Sail ho!' was the cry and all hands crowded to the rail to make out the intruder into their own private corner of hell. She looked eerie, partially dismasted and running pell-mell before the gale. On deck, there was precious little sign of life, the sails hanging in tatters and her salt-stained hull badly neglected.

She was not a comforting sight to the crew of the *Neptune's Car*. If anything, she simply underlined the loneliness and danger of their position. Her mizzen mast still stood complete, and from this flew the Stars and Stripes. However, the ensign hung upside down, a desperate final call sign of distress. As the two clippers drew closer, four men could be seen at the rail of the crippled ship, desperately gesticulating for help. Yet the *Neptune's Car* never wavered from her course, ploughing on and leaving this terrifying vision in her wake.

Seas inundate the decks of a tall ship as she wallows in heavy seas off Cape Horn. In such conditions, it was try difficult for the men to keep warm and dry.

Opposite: Men aloft handling sail off Cape Horn. The photograph gives a fine impression of how bleak things could get down in the Southern Ocean.

The *Rapid*'s turnaround

The southern winter of 1856 was a particularly brutal one off the pitch of Cape Horn. For days on end the wind shrieked out of the west, sometimes at hurricane strength, bringing with it ceaseless snowstorms. Down in that savage wasteland of darkened seas and jagged rock, the clipper fleet laboured to get clear of the dreaded cape as they battled out to San Francisco.

No ship was tried more severely by the weather than the clipper *Rapid*, commanded by Captain Winsor. She had left New York in May 1856 and had made good speed until she reached Cape Horn. Here, all progress had ceased. For weeks on end, she butted into the great grey rollers which marched relentlessly across this lonely expanse. All this time her crew were brutalised by the cold and oppressed by the gloom of this dark corner of the world. Rarely did the sun show its face and darkness closed in only a few hours after dawn. Ice formed in the rigging so thickly that it threatened to affect the clipper's stability and the crew was

compelled to struggle up the slippery ratlines to chip it away. The wind constantly roared through the rigging with a baleful howl. All of the elements seemed to be their enemy; all had forsaken them in their hour of need.

In the midst of this hell, men died. Some fell from the rigging, others simply retired to the fo'c'sle and collapsed from privation, relieved to shuffle off the earth without enduring any more suffering at the hands of this merciless tormentor. After several weeks off the Horn, ten men were dead and another ten completely incapacitated. This only left four more men to run the ship: an impossible task. Reluctantly, Captain Winsor decided to turn back to Rio. This was the only time that a clipper ever turned her back on the battle with the Horn, but Winsor was left with little choice.

As the vessel fled back across the forsaken ocean, throwing away every hard-earned mile gained over the last month of toil, Winsor perceived the sail of a clipper bound the other way. He ordered the helmsman to make a course for her and hoisted a flag

The clipper ships *Winged Arrow* and *Southern Cross* in Boston Harbour. Both of these vessels were built in Boston and were contemporaries of *Neptune's Car*.

The US ship *Red Cloud* drying her sails in harbour.

A contemporary map of Cape Horn, showing the Straits of Le Maire, through which clippers had to thread their way.

Overleaf: The *Neptune's Car* painted in Chinese waters. On her first round-the-world voyage, Joshua Patten had raced home from China loaded with tea and earned his owners a handsome profit.

of distress. Perhaps salvation was at hand. As they closed with the vessel, Captain Winsor inspected her through his telescope. Visibility was appalling and the bucking deck of the *Rapid* didn't help matters, but he swore he could make out a lady in a long dress standing on the poop, conferring earnestly with an officer. He didn't dwell on the matter, for his ship, running free, was flying past the stranger. He only noted with utter disgust that she made no attempt to stop and come to his aid. That night he wrote angrily in his log of the poor conduct of the vessel that had passed. He identified her as the clipper *Intrepid*.

However, it wasn't the *Intrepid,* it was the *Neptune's Car* – and if ever a ship had reason not to heave to and help out, it was this one. Down below in his cabin, her skipper Joshua Patten lay prostrate, unable to see or move, his body racked from time to time by dreadful fits and seizures. In the hold, her first mate writhed uncomfortably in the heavy sea, his arms and legs clapped in irons. Up on deck, the captain's wife, 19-year-old Mary Patten, had control

of the clipper and her crew of 30 men. She had consulted with the second mate about the possibility of standing by to help this desperate vessel, but the decision was taken to carry on. They had enough troubles of their own, and the captain's wife was completely focused on one thing: San Francisco and salvation for her ailing husband.

An unusual honeymoon

She had married Joshua Patten some two years before when she was only 16. Joshua was 27 and already captain of the *Neptune's Car*. No doubt she was drawn to his lively, charismatic nature, for it took a man of real drive and ambition to gain command of a clipper at such a young age. They had honeymooned aboard the clipper as she raced out to California the previous season. How different that passage had been! There had been excitement enough on that trip, but it had been of a more positive nature. Joshua had raced against three ships: the *Westward Ho!*, the *Greenfield* and the *Elizabeth S Willets*.

85

Dropping off the pilot symbolised the final break away from land at the start of a long voyage.

Mary Patten was only a girl of 19 when she set off on her second rounding of Cape Horn aboard the *Neptune's Car*.

The US clipper *Edward O'Brien*.

The race had been confined to the *Westward Ho!* and the *Neptune's Car*, and both had made passages of 101 days to San Francisco, but the *Westward Ho!* was a couple of hours faster and won the race. Hussey, the skipper of the *Westward Ho!*, was so elated that he offered to wager any sum on the next leg of the race, which took both vessels to Hong Kong. Luckily for him, there were no takers, since the *Neptune's Car* beat him by ten days. On the strength of this performance, the *Neptune's Car* had loaded tea for London and then returned to New York.

This was a lengthy and eventful honeymoon, but Mary had enjoyed it greatly and had taken to the sea like a duck to water. Joshua was a loving husband who cared for her well on the passage and took the time to teach her how to use the sextant. Mary was a sharp girl and picked it up very rapidly so that by the end of the round-the-world trip, she was as able as Joshua himself to gain a fix.

Mary was not the first clipper ship to carry a female navigator. Josiah Creesy of the *Flying Cloud* not only taught his wife to navigate, but also often relied on her to get a fix of the vessel's position. It was she who had helped him plot the *Flying Cloud*'s course on her record-breaking 89-day run to San Francisco in 1851. Nevertheless, in

Mary Patten's time, women were unquestionably at best tolerated aboard a ship. A ship was a man's world and in 1855 a woman would definitely have known her place aboard. It is telling that after their honeymoon voyage Joshua noted of his wife: 'She is uncommon handy about a ship even in weather and would doubtless be of service if a man.'

Mary was happy to join her husband for another trip around Cape Horn, and on 1 July 1856 the *Neptune's Car* made her departure from New York. She was in company with the fine clipper *Intrepid*, while the beautiful McKay-designed *Romance of the Seas* was a few hours ahead. The race was on. Yet, this time the passage down the Atlantic was punctuated by a number of unpleasant incidents. Captain Patten had been compelled to hire a new mate, William Keeler, at short notice and things were not going well.

Captain and mate
Patten was a racing sailor who loved to drive his vessel hard and, time after time, he was exasperated by Keeler's reticence in making sail. Many times he would come on deck and find the ship jogging along under shortened sail, when she should have been crowding on canvas to make the most of a favourable slant. This reticence to make sail could

Port Stanley in the Falkland Islands was a shelter for storm-battered vessels running from Cape Horn. Those deemed too expensive to repair were simply abandoned as these wrecks still in existence attest to. Mary Patten chose to ignore this isolated haven and face the Horn.

have been due to fear or may have simply been down to laziness. Sail carrying requires constant vigilance, and this can be wearing on the nerves day in, day out.

Whatever the reasons for Keeler's slackness, it caused a great deal of friction between the captain and his mate. A poor relationship between these two generally leads to an unhappy and poorly worked ship. The mate is the hub of all work that goes on aboard. In *Two Years Before the Mast*, which narrates a passage to San Francisco in 1844, Richard Dana describes how the men suffered when the relationship between the strict skipper and rather lax mate broke down. He explained: 'If the chief officer wants force, discipline slackens, everything gets out of joint, and the captain interferes continually; that makes a difficulty between them, which encourages the crew, and the whole ends in a three-sided quarrel. But our mate wanted no help from anybody, took everything into his own hands, and was more likely to encroach upon the authority of the master than to need any spurring.'

Dana continued: 'Our captain gave his directions to the mate in private, and, except in coming to anchor, getting under way, tacking, reefing topsails, and other "all-hands-work", seldom appeared in

person. This is the proper state of things; and while this lasts, and there is a good understanding aft, everything will go on well.'

Thus, captain and mate needed to work in harmony for the ship to run smoothly. Yet aboard the confined environs of a clipper, with all of its many demands, this relationship was tested day after day and even the most tolerant skipper and mate would chafe against each other's will from time to time. Usually this relationship could be patched up, but sometimes the damage was irreparable. So it proved with Keeler, and things came to a head as the clipper dashed down the South Atlantic, plunging headlong towards the Horn. Patten had taken to keeping a close eye on his recalcitrant mate and one night he stepped on deck to check that all was well. It was Keeler's watch, but he was nowhere to be found. A thorough search of the ship revealed him to be sleeping in the cook's quarters, and Patten decided to deal with the malingerer by busting him right back down to able seaman and moving him into the fo'c'sle with the rest of the crew.

Whether the two came to blows is unrecorded, but Keeler certainly reacted angrily to this move and the decision was taken to put him in irons until

90

Even on a benign day Cape Horn still looks intimidating.

the ship arrived in San Francisco. Captain Patten now stood the mate's watch and the second mate, Hare, was promoted to first mate. Hare was an excellent and able seaman, but he had very limited navigational ability. This was not a problem as long as Joshua stood watch, but the aggravation over his mate had left him not only over-worked but also overwrought.

Mary's dilemma

As the vessel neared Cape Horn, Patten began to complain of blinding headaches. Within a matter of days he was completely incapacitated and had to retire to his bunk while fever and pain racked his body. Mary nursed him as best she could, fretting all the while about what was to become of her husband and the ship. She had other problems, too. For some time she had been feeling nauseous, particularly in the mornings, and over time she deduced that she was pregnant with their first child. The Pattens were in a tight corner, and so was the vessel. She was approaching the most deadly and notorious stretch of water in the world with no skipper or mate. Her second mate could not navigate and all hands were fearful following the numerous unsettling incidents on passage.

At this point, Keeler, locked away down below, got word of the captain's predicament and sent Mary a note asking to be released so that he could take the ship to a safe haven. No doubt, Mary would have at least partly held Keeler to blame for her husband's illness; it had coincided with the stress of deposing the mate and taking on his burden of work. With this in mind, she sent word back, informing Keeler that 'if her husband did not view him as fit for work, neither did she'.

Thus galvanised, Mary and Hare agreed to push the ship on to San Francisco. Mary was to be in charge of the navigation, Hare responsible for the ship handling. So the 19-year-old girl and the inexperienced young officer prepared for any sailor's stiffest challenge, Cape Horn. Mary summoned the hands and explained the situation to the scared men; she appealed to them to help her get the ship to California. The men had taken Mary to their hearts and had little liking or faith in the bullying Keeler. They answered her with three resounding cheers of support.

It took them 18 days to weather the dreaded cape and it was during this part of the passage that the *Rapid* was sighted. It was decided that it would be almost impossible to render assistance to the

William Keeler was hoping to pull in to Valparaiso in Peru in order to escape. At the time, the town was a sleepy port, as can be seen by this illustration.

Opposite: (top) The American clipper *Starlight* in harbour. This vessel was built in 1855 in Boston and was considered a very beautiful ship. (bottom) The wharfs of San Francisco in the age of sail. The vessel in the foreground is very heavily rigged with skysails on each mast.

stricken vessel and while the *Rapid* eventually made her way to the warmer climes and gentler waters of Brazil, the *Neptune's Car* battled on bravely. Mary rarely left the deck and, when she did, she tended to her husband.

Navigation was especially challenging as a sight of the sun, required to fix their position, was rarely possible in the overcast gloom. Mary would have relied for days on end on dead reckoning, calculating the distance travelled every day and guessing at drift and leeway. This method of navigation tested the nerve of even the most experienced captain, for after several days of guessing, you can't help but feel helplessly lost. For Mary, a novice navigator with no one to reassure her, it must have been an especially testing time.

Yet she stuck to her task doggedly and eventually the relentless flogging of the vessel to gain a bit of westing ended, the yards were eased and the helm rattled down onto a more northerly course. With the wind on the beam, the big ship started to reach away at a good clip, running at full speed from those dark, desolate waters into the friendly deep blue rollers of the Pacific. All through the dark

times off Cape Horn, the men had stood by Mary and believed in her abilities. Now their faith was rewarded.

Keeler's second chance

Down in the main cabin, things were looking up, too, for Joshua was starting to show signs of recovery. He was able to eat a little and, after several more days, was even able to walk about, though he was still weak. The headaches seemed to have passed and Mary was gleeful as she noted his improvement. Joshua had no memory of the nightmare at Cape Horn, but he was deeply impressed by the conduct of his wife and his second officer. He was also concerned; he now knew that his wife was pregnant and was aware of the immense strain that had been put upon her off the Horn. It was likely this concern that persuaded him to summon Keeler to his cabin and seek a reconciliation. Keeler willingly went to speak to him and agreed to return to duty, promising good behaviour and no more trouble until they reached San Francisco. Patten agreed, although he assured Keeler that he would still face the whole weight of the law once in port.

Above: The US clipper *Abner Coburn* anchored in Bristol Bay off the coast of Alaska, where she was used in later years in the salmon industry.

Below: The 1849 gold rush transformed San Francisco from a sleepy settlement to a bustling port. Here, you can see the outer approaches to the port with a tugboat and schooner in the foreground. To the extreme left, you can see a mass of shipping, a hangover from the gold rush, when many ships were simply abandoned.

For a few days, all seemed well. Keeler took custody of the sextant and Mary took up the role of full-time nurse to her husband. Joshua continued his recovery, and there was hope in the air. After a couple of days, however, Mary became uneasy. Some instinct told her that all was not as it should be and she eventually pinned it down to the position of the sun in the sky. Her many weeks as navigator had given her an instinct for where it should be relative to the ship's course. It seemed to her that the ship was heading not so much north as north-east.

She confided her misgivings to her husband, who told her to keep an eye on things. Repeated consultation of the compass at various times confirmed her suspicions. It was evident to her that Keeler was actually steering the ship to Valparaiso, Chile. No doubt he hoped to quit the ship and escape the law there rather than face the music in San Francisco. Mary related this to Joshua, who was much disgusted with the man. He decided to confront Keeler and summoned him to his cabin. Keeler informed him curtly that he was staying as close to the desired course as he could. Joshua knew this was nonsense and moved his berth to a spot where he could keep a vigilant eye on the compass. It didn't take him long to see that his wife's suspicions were fully justified.

Again, Keeler found himself unceremoniously bundled below decks and manacled. He knew now that there was to be no redemption for him and probably cursed the young woman who had once again outflanked him. The vessel was now racing up the Pacific, hurling herself into the friendly blue rollers with exuberant abandon and throwing up great glittering walls of white water as her bow sliced through the seas. She was making good speed and on board spirits were up. Yet for Mary, this was to be a profoundly gloomy time.

The frustrating final leg

Shortly after Keeler's second departure from his post, Joshua had taken a turn for the worse. The headaches and fever had returned and, even more upsettingly, his sight had failed. Mary must have wondered if he would ever make it to San

The bustle of San Francisco's docks in the age of sail is captured in this photograph.

97

A view of San Francisco as it looked in 1849. By the time the *Neptune's Car* arrived in 1856, it had already expanded unrecognisably.

This painting of San Francisco dated 1878 shows how the gold rush town grew rapidly from its humble beginnings in the 1840s.

The clipper ship *Flying Fish* off Golden Gate. Although the Donald McKay flyer is running well, the area around San Francisco was notoriously tricky to navigate and many clippers were held up for days off the Farallon Islands, dogged by fogs and fickle breezes.

Francisco alive. She tried everything to alleviate his situation, even resorting to shaving his head in order to cool him down. Nothing seemed to help, and he spent much of the time delirious, his body racked by violent fits, which meant he often had to be physically strapped into his bunk. All the while, Mary nursed him and plotted the vessel's course to San Francisco. Here she hoped he would be able to get the medical help he so desperately required.

The run up the Pacific was uneventful, but it was as the vessel neared the Farallon Islands off the coast of San Francisco that Mary endured possibly the most frustrating part of the entire trip. The *Neptune's Car* found herself helplessly becalmed within striking distance of her destination. The men reported that they could clearly see the coast of San Francisco from the upper masts of the clipper. Yet for ten days the vessel lay utterly idle, almost within striking distance of safety. Still Joshua tossed and turned in his berth, but his fever had been alleviated by the cooler airs off San Francisco and he had regained some lucidity as the boat drifted idle, awaiting a breeze. There was some hope for her beloved husband. He was still with her.

Every calm must eventually pass and after many days of listless, helpless drifting, the vessel picked up a gentle breeze that wafted her into port. Mary saw to it that her husband was removed from the clipper with alacrity and the very best medical care that the city could provide was lavished upon him. With Mary almost five months pregnant, it was

vital that her husband recovered. She stepped off the clipper shortly after arriving in San Francisco and turned her back on the ship that had provided a home for her and her husband for more than two years. She never stepped foot aboard the gallant vessel again.

Incredibly, they had beaten the *Intrepid* into port by a clear 11 days. The *Romance of the Seas* was ahead, but it was still a mighty achievement. The *Rapid*, passed in distress off Cape Horn, had made it back to Rio where she refitted and replenished her crew. She eventually arrived in San Francisco after a truly epic passage of 225 days. There is no record of what happened to William Keeler following his arrival in San Francisco, but he would undoubtedly have faced a severe censure and at the very least would have been stripped of his mate's certificate.

Meanwhile, news of Mary's heroism had spread around the city and across America. Soon, newspapermen from as far afield as New York were clamouring to hear her story. Mary remained unmoved by this sudden celebrity and maintained that she had done no more than her duty in getting her husband to a safe port. She was approached by some of the first founders of the women's sufferance movement in the US, who were starting to push for improved rights for women. These groups rightly saw Mary as a figurehead for their movement, evidence that a woman was every bit as capable as a man. Yet Mary wanted no part of

A view of Boston waterfront as it would have looked when Mary and Joshua returned home.

it, remaining by her husband's side and praying for his recovery.

End of the fairytale

Up until now, the saga had all the elements of a fairytale, but unfortunately life doesn't always follow the script. Joshua was diagnosed at the time as having 'brain fever'. Whether this was, in modern terms, meningitis, encephalitis or even a brain tumour will never be known. The most likely explanation is that he had what is now known as central nervous system tuberculosis. This brings on the same symptoms as those reported in his case. Whatever the ailment, Joshua never recovered and Mary was forced to endure his slow decline; his moments of lucidity and clarity became less and

less frequent and he slowly came to occupy full-time a world of violent fits and nightmares.

Mary did, however, find many generous benefactors who were happy to help her out in her hour of need. After two months it was arranged that the couple should return to New York, this time catching a steamer to Panama, crossing the Isthmus and then back to the east coast and home. The journey was uneventful and the couple's arrival in New York was reported in the *Daily News* thus: 'One day last month, the people in the streets of New York observed a litter, evidently containing a sick person, carried up from the shipping to the Battery Hotel. Beside the litter walked a young creature who, but for her careworn countenance, might have been taken for a school girl.'

Shortly afterwards, a journalist from the *New York Times* visited Mary as she tended to Joshua and described the scene as follows: 'With the modesty that generally distinguishes true merit, Mrs Patten begged to be excused from speaking about herself. She said she had done no more than her duty, and as the recollection of her trials clearly pained her, we could do no otherwise than respect her feelings. Her health is very much impaired from the trials she has undergone, yet she does not spare herself in the least and is most faithful and constant in her attentions to her husband.'

Soon after this account was published, Joshua was moved to his home town of Boston, where he died five months later. He had lived long enough to witness the birth of his son, Joshua Patten

Junior, and one can only hope he retained enough lucidity to comprehend what had happened.

As for Mary, she was not destined to outlive her husband by many years. She died of tuberculosis in 1861, at the age of 24. It is highly likely she contracted it from her husband during her long days spent tending to him in the stuffy cabin of the *Neptune's Car*. Life in the days of sail was cheap, as illustrated by the ten men who died aboard the *Rapid* as she battled around Cape Horn the same year that Mary took charge of the *Neptune's Car*. Yet there is something desperately poetic about Mary Patten's tigerish devotion to her husband. Her iron will and love of her partner made an ordinary woman step up to an extraordinary task.

CHAPTER FIVE

MUTINY ABOARD THE 'WILD BOAT OF THE ATLANTIC'

It is of a flash packet,
A packet of fame.
She is bound to New York
And the Dreadnought's her name.
She is bound to the west'ard
Where the stormy winds blow.
Bound away to the west'ard,
Good Lord, let her go.
      Verse from the sea shanty 'Dreadnought'

The trouble, Captain Samuel Samuels later recalled in his memoirs, began even before the voyage started. Captain Schomberg, Liverpool's chief immigration officer, had been aboard the packet ship *Dreadnought* for about an hour, clearing her passengers for emigration to New York. Although her papers were in order, he was extremely reluctant to let the American clipper go. 'Look at this crew,' he said, gesturing at the surly rabble prowling the decks of the clipper. 'I've never seen such a set of pirates in all my life and advise you not to take them.

Think about what happened aboard the *Columbia* and I beg you to reconsider.'

Samuels winced at the mention of the *Columbia*. Her captain had been murdered in cold blood by a bunch of Liverpool packet rats, some of whom were now probably aboard his own boat. Yet Samuels remained steadfast and ushered Schomberg back to an awaiting boat. 'Never fear,' he said with a wink. 'I will draw their teeth.' The distraught officer was left with little option other than to depart with a feeling of deep foreboding in his heart.

103

Samuel Samuels: jailbird, vaudeville actor and finally master of the clipper packet *Dreadnought*.

The Black Ball Line's *New York* was a typical transatlantic packet. Clippers such as the *Dreadnought* superseded these slower vessels.

He had every reason to be afraid. The *Dreadnought* had shipped one of the most unsavoury crews that Schomberg had ever witnessed in his long and illustrious career. He shook his head. 'Those packet rats will be the end of him for sure,' he murmured as he turned his back on the clipper with an air of finality.

Samuel Samuels did not see things that way at all. He had been skipper of the *Dreadnought* ever since she was built in 1853 for the transatlantic run and the trade had taught him everything you could ever wish to know about hardship and discipline. It had become notorious for hardship; year round these tough little vessels would brave the fury of Atlantic storms and freezing waters to keep up a regular service.

Departing Liverpool with a cargo of emigrants searching for a better life, the transatlantic packet would defy the cruellest weather the Atlantic could throw at her in order to make New York. Many passengers died en route as they huddled down below. When the ship was battered by gales, the hatches had to be battened down and the screaming of the passengers from the 'tween decks was often audible over the roar of the storm. The hugely

The American clipper *AJ Fuller* under way. She shared the powerful attributes of the *Dreadnought*, which meant both ships could keep running in all but the most severe gales.

variable conditions of the North Atlantic, combined with a gruelling schedule, truly made this run one of the toughest training grounds for captain and crew. By the 1800s the trade was almost exclusively in the hands of American ship owners and evocatively named shipping lines such as the Swallow Tail Line, the Dramatic Line and the Red Cross Line.

By the 1850s the sailing packets were gradually being supplanted by steamships, and the *Dreadnought* was to be one of the last sailing ships to run this route carrying passengers, and the last vessel built for the trade by the Red Cross Line. Their ships were easily distinguishable by a huge red cross painted on the foresail. They were also notable for their extreme bad luck. By 1859, when Samuels shipped his unsavoury crew, the fleet consisted solely of the *Dreadnought*, the rest having been taken by wreck, fire and even piracy.

Many warned Samuels that his card must be marked, and after the sinking of the only other remaining Red Cross ship, the *Andrew Foster*, in 1856, he took the precaution of forbidding his family to sail with him. Yet the *Dreadnought* continued to succeed and had established herself as by far the fastest and most successful sailing ship on the transatlantic run.

The *Dreadnought*'s recipe for success
Built in 1853, she was actually not a particularly sharp ship and therefore should not have been terribly fast. What she did possess was a massive sail area and a powerful hull, which allowed a

Overleaf: **Another view of the *AJ Fuller* in dry dock, which shows off her lines to good advantage.**

A clipper ship hove to as she drops off her pilot and makes her departure from land.

daring man to push the vessel beyond what most ships could tolerate in heavy weather. As Samuels explained: 'She possessed the merit of being able to bear driving as long as her spars and sails could stand it. Many a time I have been told that the crews of other vessels, lying hove to, could see our keel as we skipped from sea to sea under every rag we dared to carry.'

Samuels also believed the big secret of the *Dreadnought*'s success was his willingness to push the vessel through the hours of darkness, when other skippers tended to snug their vessel down. The North Atlantic proved to be the ideal forum for her and, as the years rolled by, she acquired the nickname the 'wild boat of the Atlantic'.

Samuel Samuels was evidently a very talented sailor and he had enjoyed a colourful youth which included running away to sea at a young age, time in jail for jumping ship and, most bizarrely,

a stint treading the boards as part of a vaudeville act. Command of his first vessel came at the age of 21. Having gained this position 'through the hawse-pipe', you can guarantee that Samuels was a tough nut and something of a hellraiser. Aboard the *Dreadnought* he gained a reputation for the hard treatment of his crew.

Samuels had to push his crew hard since he had managed to make the *Dreadnought* the highest earning packet in the Atlantic by guaranteeing shippers that she would cross the ocean within a stipulated time. This daring business plan paid dividends, largely due to his ridiculously hard driving. In 20 passages made eastwards from New York, his ship averaged 19 days, with the quickest journey taking 13 days. No other packet could even come close to this, particularly when you bear in mind that the tall ship record, set by the Black Ball liner *James Baines*, was 12 days.

Emigrants mustered on deck as a packet prepares to depart Liverpool.

Liverpool packet rats

Now Samuels faced a fresh challenge. His speedy passages had come at a price to his crew and there was talk of tough treatment. This had come to the attention of Liverpool's 'packet rats'. These sailors were a special breed born from generations of Scousers working in the transatlantic trade. These men were famed for their toughness as much as for their laziness. The signing-on terms for a transatlantic crossing were that seamen got paid their wages in advance. This meant that in their terms they were 'working a dead horse' on the passage. Having already had their pay prior to departure, they had little or no motivation to work hard. Although they were very experienced sailors who were handy when it came to the essentials of sail handling, they would do little more than was required for their own safety and progress to the next port.

Samuels describes them thus: 'The Liverpool sailors were not easily demoralised. They were the toughest class of men in all respects. They could stand the worst weather, food and usage and put up with less sleep, more rum and harder knocks than any other sailors. They would not serve in any other trade and they had not the slightest idea of morality or honesty. These rascals could never be brought to subjection by moral persuasion.'

The packet rats had a tendency to dominate and subjugate other crew members. Samuels often noted how a packet rat would come aboard having spent his advance on some drunken spree. Barefoot and ragged, he seemed ill-prepared for the lacerating cold of a transatlantic crossing. As the voyage progressed, Samuels would notice that the sailor in question would gradually acquire more and more layers of clothes, while other sailors who were not part of the 'packet rat' fraternity would lose theirs.

Emigrants say their final goodbye to England. For many it would be their last sight of their homeland.

Brutal tactics were required to make them work and under men like Samuels they got more than their fair share. So much so that by 1859 many regulars on the Atlantic run had a score to settle with Captain Samuels.

A number of the toughest seamen had formed themselves into a group known as the 'Bloody Forty', led by three Liverpool hard men: Sweeney, Casey and Finnegan. This gang shipped aboard the *Dreadnought* in 1859 with the express intention of teaching Samuels a lesson. Their plot was public knowledge in Liverpool and many assumed that Samuels would discharge the crew rather than be fool enough to go to sea with this band of cut-throats.

Dreadnought's skipper saw things differently, however. He knew he had to confront this problem head on and was confident he could deal with his crew. Backing down, he felt, would simply defer the problem. His confidence in his ability to deal with

the troublemakers was bolstered by the fact that he was a noted shot with a pistol. Samuels also never trod the decks without his faithful dog, Wallace, at his side. Wallace was a huge Newfoundland, and was utterly devoted to his master.

Prior to departure, Samuels had the crew empty out their kitbags and any knives carried had their points snapped off. There was much grumbling among the crew at this, so the captain determined to lay down the law. Addressing them, he said: 'The saucy manner you crew just assumed is insulting and you know it. Finnegan, you and Casey have sailed with me before so you know what to expect.'

He continued: 'I know you are the ringleaders of the Bloody Forty, 30 of whom I see before me now. I know you have banded yourselves together and have taken an oath to clip the wings of the bloody old *Dreadnought* and give the skipper a swim. You think that the lid of Davy Jones' locker has been open long enough for me. Now you see that I know and do not fear you, but am glad to have such men that I think I can teach a lesson to for the rest of your life.'

With that, the *Dreadnought* sailed and an uneasy truce settled over the ship that lasted until the following morning. Samuels had already noted how shoddily much of the work was being done by the truculent crew and the sullen manner in which they worked suggested that it would only take a small spark for violence to flare.

The provocation

Samuels decided to force the situation and, while the crew were at dinner, he got his chance: 'I was walking the quarter-deck watching the course, and noticing that the man at the wheel was not steering steadily, I said, "Steer steady!" He made no reply. "Did you hear me speak to you, sir?" I inquired. "I am steering steady," he answered in a sullen manner. The impertinent tone of his voice caused me to jump towards him. He attempted to draw his sheath-knife. Seeing my danger, I struck the man, knocking him senseless leeward of the wheel. Wallace, my dog, then took charge of him,

and kept his fore paws on his chest. I took the knife from him, and called the officers to handcuff him. He was then put in the after-house, and locked up.'

All remained quiet for a couple of hours. The hands returning from lunch were initially unaware of what had happened, but gradually news filtered through and angry snarls were heard forward. At this point the hands were ordered to trim the mainsail and refused, demanding that the man in irons be released. The refusal amounted to mutiny, and Samuels headed to his cabin to arm himself. As he did, the crew raced forward to gather their own. The passengers aboard were utterly terrified. Samuels ordered them below and went to the fo'c'sle to see what was brewing.

As he approached the fo'c'sle, the men rushed out armed with their knives, clearly with the intention of rushing Samuels and overpowering him. They were stopped in their tracks by Samuels and the barrels of his two pistols trained unwavering on them.

Samuels again takes up the story: 'With a pistol in each hand and a cutlass at my waist I stood immovable. Not a man dared to come within 12 ft

A whaler with fishing vessels off the Labrador coast. Icebergs were a very real threat for vessels like the *Dreadnought* in the transatlantic trade, as the *Titanic* demonstrated so dramatically a few decades later.

Two rare photographs of the American clippers *Abner Coburn* (above) and *Panay* (right) under way. Like the *Dreadnought*, they were fuller lined than the earlier extreme clippers and it was these mighty wooden vessels that saw out the twilight of American commercial sail.

of me, knowing that another step forward would seal his doom. My pistol practice had been heard of and I was a dead shot with both hands and my pistols were on a hair trigger. During a momentary lapse in the clamour I said: "Men, you have found your master." Finding that they would not listen to what I had to say, I retreated. With a yell they rushed forward and pointing my pistols at them, I said: "The first man that advances another step dies."'

This seemed to have the desired effect, as the crew backed off and barricaded themselves forward, refusing to work. Several stand-offs

resolved nothing and, with the wind freshening, things were looking bleak. By this time many of the passengers had had enough and begged Samuels to put into the Irish port of Queenstown (modern-day Cobh), some eight miles distant. Samuels refused, stating that the *Dreadnought* was bound for New York, not Queenstown. The stand-off remained, but the crew had no access to the ship's stores, and Samuels made it clear that if any of the mutineers

Overleaf: The clipper ship *Thomas Reed* off the San Francisco coast.

112

stepped abaft the mainmast, they would be shot dead.

So far, Samuels had been fortunate that the weather had remained fair, but the following day the breeze started to freshen. The royals were going to need taking in. 'Take in the royals,' Samuels sang out loudly, and was met with loud replies of 'go to hell' from the crew. Fortunately the officers were able to take in the royals and topgallants, but Samuels knew they would not be able to handle the lower sails and all through the night he was obliged to carry on in the most terrifying manner as squalls bore down on the *Dreadnought*. She was truly living up to her reputation as the wild boat of the Atlantic.

The following morning, the overwrought passengers had just about had enough. They begged for Samuels to go forward and make peace with the crew. He refused, whereupon some swore they would go forward and feed the hungry men themselves.

Going aloft to trim the sails was a vital part of a crew's duty. The refusal of the *Dreadnought*'s crew to do so was serious dereliction of their duty.

A night scene off Maine.

This photo of the *Jabez Howes* gives a good idea of the size and height of a clipper's spars. Without a crew, a clipper was totally unmanageable.

Samuels explained in no uncertain terms the folly of their plan: 'If the mutineers conquer me they will scuttle the ship, after having committed the greatest outrages on those whom you hold most dear; and at night, while you are asleep, the hatches will be battened down and the ship sunk, while they will take to the boats, expecting to be picked up by a passing ship, and making up stories as have frequently been told – that the ship had sprung a leak and sunk, leaving them the only survivors. These men know now that they have subjected themselves to years in prison.

'You see, therefore, that these men intend to take my life and to escape in the boats rather than subject themselves to such penalty. I mean to bring them to subjection through hunger, and I forbid you to give them food or aid them in any way in their mutinous conduct.'

Crisis point

By now the crew had gone 56 hours without food and Samuels realised that a crisis was imminent. Two crew members came aft and surrendered to the skipper, which was a positive sign. His next step

117

New York in the days of sail. This picture dates from 1883, the year that the Brooklyn Bridge was opened.

was to persuade a group of German passengers to help him out. They agreed and were armed with iron bars from the hold. Samuels knew from the defecting mutineers that the crew planned to rush the galley. At 3.45 am he headed forward with his dog to bargain with the crew.

'When Wallace reached the forecastle a deep growl indicated that someone was hidden forward of it,' Samuels recounted. 'I knew Casey and Sweeney would lead the attack and so it proved. I was proceeding cautiously with pistol in hand to the edge of the house when they both jumped out at me with arms raised and knives in hand ready to strike. In an instant I levelled my pistol at Casey and

the dog jumped at Sweeney's throat. Casey, seeing the danger, backed up to the forecastle scuttle while the other two men shouted down to the forecastle scuttle: "Jump up, boys! Let's murder him now!'"

A plan had been put in place for some of the men to sneak round the other side of the fo'c'sle and surprise Samuels, but he in turn had stationed the German passengers to put a stop to this – which they did by beating the mutineers with their iron bars.

Samuels' account continued: 'Seeing themselves defeated and me reinforced, the men retreated to the starboard side forward where I held them at bay with my pistol levelled. "Death to anyone who dares

The bows of the 'wild boat of the Atlantic' hang over the wharf of South Street, New York.

advance!" I shouted. "I will give you one moment to throw your knives overboard." Finnegan now spoke up: "You shall be the first to go, you damned psalm singing bastard."' The rest of the crew, however, had started to see things differently and sought a bargain of returning to work provided the captain did not prosecute them for mutiny on arrival in New York.

However, Samuels said: 'I will make no bargain with you. Throw your knives overboard and get back to work.' Sensing the will of their master, one of the crew piped up: 'Well, boys, it's no use. He is too much for us, here goes mine.' And his knife flew over the side. The rest followed suit, leaving Finnegan and Casey isolated and hopeless. Finnegan was ordered to apologise and on refusing was clapped in irons below.

The men were promptly assigned the unpleasant task of scrubbing the decks. Their spirits utterly broken, they turned to and scrubbed with a will. After several hours of diligent scrubbing and polishing, Samuels called the crew aft. 'We seem

A whaler carrying low sail in anticipation of bad weather. There must be a big blow expected as the upper yards have been sent down to improve stability.

to have reached an understanding,' he said, with admirable understatement. Only after this was the hungry crew allowed some food. The mutiny was quelled and, for the rest of the voyage, the behaviour of all was exemplary.

By the time the lights of New York hove into view, Samuels was in a quandary as to what to do with his crew. Ultimately he opted to do nothing, simply imploring them to think about their lives and what they were doing. As the crew departed, he was treated to three rousing cheers from a desperate band of men. The wild boat of the Atlantic and her forceful master had finally tamed the Bloody Forty.

Rudderless in mid-ocean

For the next three years Samuels continued to ply the Atlantic aboard the *Dreadnought*, but his adventures were far from over. The next catastrophe to fall upon his ship would not only confirm that Samuels was a consummate sailor, but would also finally split him and his proud command asunder in the most dramatic of circumstances.

Two tugs attempting to aid a disabled clipper. This illustrates the difficulties faced by the French merchantman endeavouring to rescue the *Dreadnought*.

Repairs to the rudder were undertaken in Horta, Faial.

The *Dreadnought* was working her way across a stretch of the Atlantic nicknamed the 'devil's blow hole' when she was battered by winds far stronger than any Samuels had experienced previously. He had been almost a decade in charge of the *Dreadnought* and never once felt the need to heave her to, but now he knew he must. As skipper and crew waited for the right moment to brace up her mighty mainyard, the old clipper shipped a huge sea that hurled her captain forward and left him senseless under a pile of spare spars. One leg was broken and also a wrist, his head was badly gashed and he was half drowned. During a lull in the storm, the crew succeeded in extricating him from the pile of spars and took him below.

Samuel's main problem now was that the only person even vaguely resembling a doctor aboard the ship was him. Most vessels relied on the captain and a trusty copy of the ship's medical journal to come up with a solution to any problem. Thus Samuels set about setting his own leg with the help of the steward and two crew.

In retirement, Samuels took up yacht racing. In 1866 he commanded the *Henrietta* in the first offshore race of note (above) and, 21 years later, he skippered the *Dauntless* in a transatlantic race against the *Coronet*.

A desperate jury repair to a tall ship's steering gear. The wheel was often damaged as it was vulnerable to following seas. This made helming in heavy seas a real test of nerve.

A dramatic depiction of an unknown clipper ship battling with immense seas similar to those which disabled the *Dreadnought*.

Three strong men were unable to set the leg back in place, not realising that you had to bend the limb to relax the muscles. Half mad with pain, Samuels made the decision to self-amputate and prepared a knife and tourniquet. Thankfully he was dissuaded by the second mate, who had some limited medical knowledge, and the leg was simply lashed up and left. The second mate had actually come below to report that the *Dreadnought*'s rudder had been ripped off and the vessel was drifting helplessly. Samuels spent an agonising night being thrown around his cabin, all the while aware that his vessel was in dire straits.

The following morning the storm had abated, but the situation was still grim. Samuels was confined to his cabin, but determined to command the ship as best he could from there. He promptly sent for the carpenter to discuss a jury rudder, only to be informed that the man had died the previous night. This was a severe blow, and from thereon Samuels was to know little but adversity. A jury rudder was built, but it somehow ended up being lost over the side before it could be fixed into position.

Down below, helpless in his cabin, Samuels seethed. There was great frustration aboard as the vessel was only 360 miles from the island of Faial in the Azores and there was a favourable breeze blowing her in that direction – if only the *Dreadnought* could be persuaded to turn her nose that way. All attempts failed and, several days later, a French merchantman came upon the helpless clipper and agreed to tow her around so that she could run before the favourable breeze.

A full day of attempts failed and, at the end of it, the Frenchman departed and Samuels fired his first mate. He now determined to sail backwards to Faial in the light winds, while the rudder was repaired. After 180 miles of running in this unorthodox manner, a second jury rudder was completed and this time fitted successfully. Two weeks after the accident, the battered vessel dropped her anchor at Faial and Samuel sought a surgeon. At the time, his left leg was two inches shorter than his right and he engaged on a brutal course of resetting and stretching to repair the mangled limb.

He also remained in command of the *Dreadnought* and fought hard with the insurers who stated that the vessel must have all of her cargo removed in order to replace the

A grey day in the Atlantic; an officer ventures out of the deckhouse and braves the elements.

rudder. This was due to the lack of a dry dock and was going to prove extremely costly to the owners. Samuels refused and instead trimmed the ship well down by the head so that the sternpost was almost clear of the water and the new rudder could be dropped on with ease, saving the vessel's owners a great deal of money. The *Dreadnought*, with Samuels still aboard, then carried on her voyage to New York, arriving without further incident. Samuels found himself confined to his bed for the next year as his mangled leg healed. It was his last passage on the *Dreadnought*.

Nevertheless, this was far from the end of his seafaring days. Samuels, along with his compatriot Joshua Slocum, was one of the few deep-water sailing men who switched their attention from racing clipper ships to racing yachts. He found further fame when he was asked to skipper the *Henrietta* in her 1866 race across the Atlantic against the *Fleetwing* and *Vesta*. This was the first offshore yacht race of any note and it is fitting that a veteran of the Atlantic packet service should have won. He later endured disappointment when in command of the *Dauntless* in her race against the *Cambria* from Queenstown to New York in 1870. He almost fully recovered from his horrific leg injury and professed to only a slight limp in later years.

Wrecked near Cape Horn

The final irony for the *Dreadnought* came when she was wrecked in 1869. By the mid-1860s it was clear that the days of the sailing packet were over and the *Dreadnought* was moved to the New York–San Francisco run to make way for the steamers. In 1869 she was heading for the Le Maire Straits near Cape Horn when she found herself becalmed beneath the dark, foreboding coastline of Tierra del Fuego. A heavy sea was rolling in and, to everyone's horror, a strong current was setting the ship inshore.

The ship lay motionless, all sails set in the eerie calm. There was no possibility of anchoring as the coastline was sheer and plunged immediately down to unfathomable depths. As the *Dreadnought* closed with the inhospitable shore, a desperate attempt was made to pull her off using the ship's boats, but it proved fruitless. This legendary vessel, veteran of a thousand storms, slowly drifted onto the rocks and into her grave in the most prosaic manner imaginable. She was slowly dashed to pieces by the relentless Cape Horn swell.

125

CHAPTER SIX

THE GREAT CHINA TEA RACE OF 1866

Donald MacKinnon fiddled distractedly with a giant sheaf of papers and glanced longingly out of the window at the glistening waters of the Pagoda anchorage, desperately hoping that the clerk would stamp his paperwork and liberate him from this purgatory. The Chinese method of clearing customs was a civil servant's dream and, in the midday heat of Foochow, it was unbearable. MacKinnon looked across at George Innes, who was enduring the same torment, and wondered when he was going to blow his top. Not long, he reckoned.

The pair commanded the clippers *Taeping* and *Serica* respectively and as veteran skippers should have been calm in the face of this rigmarole. Yet departure day was a tense one for any captain and when you were one of the first boats away in the prestigious annual China tea race, you had every reason to be nervous. Both skippers were desperate to be the first ship back to London with new teas, and they had already had to endure the galling sight of the beautiful new clipper *Ariel* slip out of the Pagoda anchorage in the first light of dawn. However, since then, something else had happened that had turned tension into rage.

George Innes paced around the customs office. He was trembling with fury and MacKinnon knew he was on the verge of apoplexy. Ever since the vessels had begun loading tea, Captain Robinson of the *Fiery Cross* had taken every opportunity to wind up Innes. Now he had gone too far and Innes seemed to be reaching incandescent rage. The customs clerk returned some of his bills of lading with a quizzical look, and something snapped. Hurling his papers to the ground, Innes stormed out, leaving MacKinnon to glance apologetically at the perplexed customs officer. He too was vexed, though.

The Pagoda anchorage, Foochow, in 1866. The tea clippers are lined up awaiting their cargo. Pictured left to right: the *Black Prince*, the *Fiery Cross*, the *Taitsing*, the *Taeping* and the *Flying Spur*.

Another view of the Pagoda anchorage, as it looked in 1866.

A tea plantation in the Chinese interior.

When it came to the China tea race, even loading up your boat was a competition against your rivals. The shippers had favoured the lovely *Ariel*, which was fair enough, but it looked set to be a dead heat between the next three vessels: the *Serica*, *Taeping* and *Fiery Cross*. By rights, they should all have left on the same tide. Yet at midday, while the other two skippers were rowed ashore to clear customs, a tug had sidled up alongside the *Fiery Cross* and towed her down the Min River to the sea. Customs hadn't been cleared and bills of lading were left unsigned, but the *Fiery Cross* was gone, leaving George Innes on the verge of babbling insanity.

Innes had a special reason to be aggrieved. The previous year he had raced Robinson back from Foochow, the clippers leaving on the same tide. Some 16,000 miles later, they had arrived in the English Channel with only a few miles separating them, but it had been the *Serica* leading. Somehow, Robinson on the *Fiery Cross* had sniffed out a tug that had towed her up to London ahead of her rival. Much bitterness had ensued, as the tea shippers paid out an extra ten shillings per ton of tea to the winner of the race. This added up to a great deal of money. In addition to this, the crews of both boats had bet an entire month's wages against each other on the outcome, and the unsatisfactory finish meant emotions were running high.

Out to sea

Customs cleared, the tide now dictated that the *Serica* and *Taeping* wouldn't be able to leave until early the following morning. While Innes stewed, the *Fiery Cross* was making progress down the Min River. The Pagoda anchorage was about 15 miles from the open sea and this first part of the journey was very beautiful. Steep, lush hills dropped right down to the water's edge, their peaks often shrouded in soft mists. The lower slopes were terraced to a dizzying height with the tea crop. Now and again a small village or a temple, clinging to the hillside, would punctuate the natural beauty of the place.

It was a breathtaking departure point. Yet Richard Robinson paid little attention to the scenery. He was on his mettle on this treacherous river. A couple of miles downstream, he approached the Mingan Pass and the river narrowed to a gorge. The tide would race through at seven knots on the flood. If you grounded here, your ship was at the mercy of the tide and the Chinese wreckers, who could strip a stricken vessel in a matter of hours.

The *Serica* drying her sails prior to departure. She had been launched from the same yard as the *Taeping* in the same year, but was always slightly slower.

Monsoon season in SE Asia can bring dramatic and violent storms, as this painting illustrates.

A modern day view of the Min River at the Pagoda anchorage.

The Min River was a very picturesque departure point for the tea clippers.

131

With three victories in the tea race in her first five seasons afloat, *Fiery Cross* had dominated the tea trade for the previous five seasons, but by 1866, the newer vessels were threatening to steal her crown and only her hard driving captain was keeping her competitive.

As the *Fiery Cross* approached the wreck of the clipper *Childers*, which had met this precise fate, the crew focused on another ship ahead, sheering about in the current, evidently anchored. 'Why, it's the *Ariel*!' Robinson's mate exclaimed, and so it was. The *Ariel* had suffered some problem with her tug, had been forced to anchor hastily and had missed the tide over the bar. Captain Robinson chuckled; he knew that the *Fiery Cross* was two feet shallower than the *Ariel* and would get across the bar with no trouble.

On the deck of the *Ariel*, Captain John Keay eyed the approaching ship with dismay. After a trying few hours, things were getting worse. As the *Fiery Cross* came alongside, Captain Robinson doffed his hat to Keay in a mocking farewell. Across the water, three derisive cheers for the *Ariel* resounded lustily from the crew of the *Fiery Cross*. Keay and his crew were left fuming as their rival swept by.

The following morning the *Ariel* finally towed out to sea, but now she had company. Both the *Serica* and *Taeping* had caught her up. In the morning haze,

the trio traded tacks in the fluky breeze, trying to gain an advantage. It was 16,000 miles to London, but even at this stage, every yard counted. About 24 hours later, the *Taitsing*, under Captain Nutsford, finished loading and was towed downriver in pursuit. The rest of the fleet was not far behind, but the race was to be between these five.

The captains and their ships
The leading ships were well matched. The *Ariel* was probably the favourite as she was brand-new, freshly launched from the Clyde yard of Robert Steele in Greenock. Many a discerning sailor had eyed her with admiration as she lay at the Pagoda anchorage awaiting her cargo. She was slightly larger than her rivals and incredibly elegant. Her low black hull gleamed in the sunlight, her graceful sheer accentuated by a gilt riband which ran along her deck line. Her counter stern was far daintier and more cut away than any other clipper.

In fact, when hard-pressed on the passage out, she had utterly terrified her crew by scooping up

A painting of an unknown tea clipper slashing through the China Sea. Close inspection of her deck layout and sail plan suggests the only likely candidate is the beautiful *Ariel*.

water over this beautiful counter and threatening to wash her helmsman away. Captain Keay kept very quiet about that, but he nursed doubts about her safety in a big following sea.

In contrast to the newcomer, the *Taeping* and *Serica* were both tried and tested, being three years old and, like Ariel built by Robert Steele. The *Serica* had won the 1864 tea race and lost out by the narrowest of margins in 1865. The *Taeping* was very fast, but a serious dismasting had kept her out of the first flight for two seasons. She had run home from Hong Kong with a favourable monsoon in the astonishing time of 88 days the year before. Now was her chance.

The *Taitsing*, meanwhile, was a new ship and an unknown quantity, but the *Fiery Cross*… well, everyone knew about the *Fiery Cross*. She was six years old and had won the China race in four of the past five seasons. She was old now, but still the boat to beat.

The fastest ship on earth was nothing without a good skipper and, despite several of them being

rather out of temper on departure, these were men at the peak of their game. Captain Robinson's antics had succeeded in enraging everyone, and this was partly because all knew they could not afford to let him get away from them. He was too sharp for that; a man of incredible energy, Robinson wrung every last ounce of speed out of his ship. A passenger who travelled aboard the *Fiery Cross* with Robinson in command voiced his utter amazement at the chaos of ropes and sails that strewed the decks as Robinson charged around like a man on springs, trimming the yards frantically to get that extra tenth of a knot out of his ship.

Captain Keay of the *Ariel* was a very different man. A quiet, taciturn Scot, he raced his ship in a very scientific manner and had a special weighted box on wheels which he would use to adjust the trim of the *Ariel* to suit the conditions. Unlike Robinson, he was a meticulous man who enjoyed order aboard. He wasn't afraid to take a risk to get ahead and, with the twitchy *Ariel* under his command, he was going to need nerves of steel. He enjoyed a strong rivalry

133

D.M.LITTLE.

The *Ariel* and *Taeping* were both built by Robert Steele in Greenock and were probably the favourites in the 1866 race.

Captain John Keay of the *Ariel* (above) and Captain Donald MacKinnon of the *Taeping* (above right) had a rivalry dating back to the 1850s.

The *Ariel* under a very heavy press of sail, including many of her 'flying kites', gives an excellent impression of speed as she slashes through the water.

A contemporary advert for China tea. The advert stresses that this is for the sought-after 'first crop' Pekoe and Congou teas from Foochow.

with his fellow Scot MacKinnon, a native of the small island of Tiree and a man of similar temperament and drive. Back in the 1850s and early 1860s these two had commanded the rivals *Ellen Rodger* and *Falcon*, the dominant vessels in the trade until the *Fiery Cross* had turned up. Now they commanded newer, faster vessels and were determined to assert their superiority.

Fiery Captain Innes of the *Serica* was a daredevil and a drinker. He'd been in the China trade for many years and knew every trick in the book. A short cut in the China Seas held no fear for him. So much so that he had rammed his previous command, the *Lady Grant*, onto a reef and lost her. Captain Nutsford of the *Taitsing* knew Innes very well as Nutsford had been mate on the *Serica* on her previous voyage.

Both were capable of pushing their ships to the limit as illustrated by this anecdote from Nutsford: One night the *Serica* was tearing along before a gale under a tremendous press of sail, the ship's very fabric groaning under the strain. With the wind increasing, Nutsford went below to ask Innes if it might be wise to reduce sail a little. Innes, who was taking a nap, answered sleepily: 'Can ye still see the

lee cathead?' (The cathead is on the bow – if you can't see it, the ship is half submerged.) Nutsford answered in the affirmative, upon which Innes sank back into slumber, murmuring: 'She's a'right then.'

All five of these skippers firmly believed they could win the race. The long voyage would be about constant vigilance. Generally, in the first leg down the China Sea, the skipper would lash a cane chair to the break of the poop and take the occasional cat nap. Even after that, there would be no real rest until London. Keay, for one, had his entire cabin jammed full of tea chests as he sought to get some extra weight aft.

The challenges of sailing China clippers

Handling a China clipper was a challenge in itself. The captain was in charge of a 200 ft racing machine, setting around 30,000 square feet of canvas on anything up to 40 different sails. In addition to the regular sails, a clipper carried innumerable 'flying kites', or stunsails, on light spars. These sails were forever being taken in and reset, so there was no let-up for captain or crew.

China clippers were not like normal ships in the way they handled squalls either. The standard approach on any tall ship was to bear away and run before a squall until its ferocity was spent. Woe betide the clipper captain who took this method. The ships were so fine-lined that if you turned away from the wind during a squall, the vessel would generally lay over with her rudder half out the water until the sea started pouring over the gunwales.

A story told in fo'c'sles of the time was how the

Overleaf (left): **On deck aboard a clipper ship in heavy weather. Many of the tea clippers had very low bulwarks, leaving crew exposed in heavy seas.**

Overleaf (right) **The *Salamis* sits bolt upright in dry dock awaiting a fresh coat of anti foul. This beautiful clipper ship was built in 1875. She was the iron sister to the attractive *Thermopylae* and was almost as fast. Although built for the tea trade, the *Salamis* never carried a cargo of tea, but was diverted into the Australian trade where she made a reputation for herself as the fastest iron clipper in the wool fleet. She was wrecked in the South Seas in 1905.**

Above: The China trader *Thomas Blyth* entering Hong Kong. Smaller clippers such as this were no match for flyers such as *Ariel* and *Fiery Cross*.

Left: Sail handling aboard a racing clipper was an endless and demanding job, with the yards requiring constant adjustment. Falling from aloft was a continous risk and many sailors perished in this manner.

Above: A dramatic depiction of the kind of Chinese war junk that operated in the China Sea during the time of the clipper ships.

Right: The monsoon weather could be very unpredictable with extremely severe squalls often sweeping in almost out of nowhere. Yet it was the typhoon that was feared by all sailors traversing the China Sea. There is no difference between a typhoon and a hurricane except its location, as typhoon derives from the Japanese term for a severe revolving storm. In this picture a vessel scuds, helplessly before the typhoon. The masses of reefs and islands in the China Sea made running before the typhoon even more fraught with risk.

Men aloft changing sails in preparation for the doldrums. Tall ships carried a separate suit of older, worn sails for the light airs of the tropics as there was so much chafe as the sails flogged. This meant that many hours were spent aloft switching sails around.

A clipper ship running well in the trades. Trade wind sailing was often a truly joyous period of a voyage while the hard driving of the ships made for exhilarating sailing.

hugely dignified and vastly experienced Captain Robert Deas had been given command of the very sharp clipper *Titania*. Although very competent, Deas was not used to handling flighty clippers. Faced with his first serious blow some days after departure, Deas promptly ordered the helm to be put down so she could run before the squall. The clipper proceeded to lay her gunwale under the water and tear along out of control at an undignified angle. All this time, her stately captain clung to the rail, pipe clenched between his teeth, as he tried to maintain his regal demeanour. Shortly afterwards, the *Titania* was dismasted.

The trick was to luff up and 'shake the wind out of her'. This is all very well in theory, but anyone who has luffed a yacht or dinghy will appreciate the nerve it takes to fire a 1,000-ton boat into the wind and let the sails flog for an indeterminate amount of time. Imagine the thundering of canvas! The utmost care also had to be taken to prevent the boat getting caught aback; otherwise she might lose her spars or worse.

Navigation was also a nightmare. The azure waters of the China Sea are dotted with low islands fringed with palm trees and powdery white sand. In places it is breathtakingly beautiful, but beneath the water the beauty turns treacherous. The shallow waters are studded with reefs that you have to thread your way through. At the time, many of them were unmarked or in the wrong place on the chart. Shoals were often named after the ship that left her bones there and were a constant reminder of the ever-present dangers of these waters. In 1866 the Lammermuir Bank was still marked with the sun-bleached stump of its namesake's mast. These were gravestones that marked the route down to the Sunda Strait.

Local knowledge was everything and a daring skipper could con his way through a shoal with a man looking out from the topmast, saving himself several days in the process. It took nerves of steel. If you got it wrong in the narrow reef-studded passages, the outcome was often fatal as Chinese pirates gave no quarter to a stricken crew. The previous year the clipper *Childers* was attacked after grounding on her way to Foochow. All crew were murdered with the exception of the carpenter who jumped overboard and clung to the rudder. After looting, the pirates burnt the ship. The glare attracted a gunboat, which rescued the carpenter.

If all that wasn't bad enough, the racers left in June when the south-west monsoon started to take charge. This meant a tough beat down the China Seas. With monsoon season came fearsome squalls and torrents of rain. Donald MacKinnon knew about the power of the monsoon. Two years previously he had been sailing the *Taeping* up the China Sea when he had been badly battered by the monsoon and forced to limp into Hong Kong dismasted. He wanted no such disasters this time around and progress was good as he nursed his ship down the coast of Cochin China (modern-day Vietnam), working the land and sea breezes to his advantage. The trick here was to time your tacks so that you stood into the coast just as the land breeze kicked in, which was often quite late in the day. It took great finesse to get it absolutely right.

Manoeuvring for position

On 7 June the *Taeping* was in touch with the *Ariel* and the following day her crew were deeply gratified to cross tacks with the *Fiery Cross* off the low-lying Paracel Islands. From here, the racers crossed to the Borneo coast and threaded the treacherous Gaspar Strait between Borneo and Sumatra. After being caught by the *Taeping*, the *Fiery Cross* had regained her lead as she passed through the Sunda Strait – the entry to the Indian Ocean. The *Ariel* and *Taeping* were next through, two days behind, and they were followed by the *Serica* and *Taitsing*, four and eight days respectively behind the leader.

Out in the Indian Ocean, life became easier for the clippers and their crews. The skipper might even permit himself to go below and sleep. Under the benign influence of the south-east trades the clippers could spread their wings, skimming across the seas, logging 300 nautical miles and more a day as they sped home. Aboard the *Fiery Cross*, Robinson was pushing on like a lunatic. He was actually three days ahead of the chasing pack as he passed Mauritius. The *Serica* and *Taitsing* seemed to be out of the running by now, dropping several hundred miles behind the leaders. However, as the *Fiery Cross*

Overleaf: **The *Taeping* running before a freshening wind. She was always noted for her unusual speed in very light airs and managed to give the *Fiery Cross* the slip in the doldrums.**

The *Taitsing* made the quickest running of the whole fleet as she raced past the Azores.

A pilot gig approaching the pilot cutter. This illustrates the tricky job a pilot boat crew had in rough conditions.

Dawn of 6 September 1866 revealed two mysterious racers running up the English Channel.

closed with the Cape of Good Hope, Robinson took a gamble that didn't pay off. He opted to stand in close to the coast to make use of the Agulhas current. The tactic backfired and the wind died. Further offshore, the *Ariel* and *Taeping* enjoyed more wind and closed in on the veteran racer.

Past the cape, the *Taeping* got a good slant of wind and took the lead so long guarded by the *Fiery Cross*. Further back in the pack, the *Serica* started to fly and passed the *Ariel* to take third place for a short while, before dropping back again. By the time the equator had been crossed, the *Ariel*, *Taeping* and *Fiery Cross* were all level, with the *Serica* a couple of hundred miles behind. Meanwhile, the *Taitsing* was rapidly closing the gap to the leaders. Bringing a breeze up behind her, she was making the best time of the fleet.

On 9 August there was much excitement aboard the *Fiery Cross* when a sail was spotted on the starboard beam. To the trained eye of the sailor it was clear that she was one of the China fleet, and there was frenzied speculation as to which one. It didn't take long to work out that she was the *Taeping* and the pair remained in company, racing side by side for eight days. There was very little to choose between them. The tension aboard both vessels was palpable and spirits were high. Both were fairly certain they were at the head of the tea fleet and to race along so evenly matched was perfection itself.

On 17 August, however, the *Taeping* finally gave her rival the slip. At the time both boats were lying listlessly in a flat calm, about half a mile separating them. As the crew of the *Fiery Cross* eyed their rival, they saw the sea nearby darken and ruffle as a gentle cat's paw played with the water. The *Taeping*'s sails gently filled and she ghosted off, gathering speed as the wind filled in. Yet the breeze missed the *Fiery Cross* altogether and the ship was left sweltering in a clock calm as the crew, cursing volubly, watched their rival disappear, sail after sail, over the horizon.

As the ships raced up to the Azores, some magnificent fluke of the winds seemed to be pushing them together. The *Taitsing* continued to gain on the leaders, the *Fiery Cross* again caught and overhauled the *Taeping* and the *Serica* was level, too. The result was that, with the exception of the *Taitsing*, all the ships passed the island of Flores on the same day. The order was the *Ariel*, followed by the *Fiery Cross*, the *Taeping* and *Serica*, with the *Taitsing* passing the island 48 hours later.

From here, south-westerly winds hurried the racers to the Western Approaches. All aboard were in high spirits and it's likely that each skipper believed he had won the race. Robinson and

Overleaf: The *Taitsing* off the Chinese coast. She was a new ship in 1866 and her maiden passage home from China was to be the fastest of her entire tea-carrying career. Her owner, James Findlay, also owned the *Serica* and must have wondered why his newer, larger ship was beaten by his older one.

Unloading tea in London Dock. This illustration captures the bustle of activity and haste when a tea-laden ship arrived with her precious goods.

Opposite top: A vessel about to be taken under tow by a tug. The securing of a tow was to prove very important to the outcome of the 1866 race.

Opposite bottom: A tug runs alongside a tall ship bargaining a price to be towed up to London.

MacKinnon may have had their doubts after their lengthy duel near the equator, but the rest probably thought they had done enough.

Prior to 1866, the fastest passage back from Foochow against the monsoon had been 101 days, set by the *Fiery Cross*. All five clippers were on target to equal or better this and logic dictated they would be first home. They ran on joyously now, spreading every stitch of canvas and flying before the big Atlantic swells, which tumbled them home to London Dock.

On the home stretch

The morning of 3 September found the *Ariel* running hard before strong south-westerlies, one reef in the mainsail and full topsails. It was a helter-skelter run up the North Atlantic, with the south-westerly breezes kicking up a big following swell that threatened to overwhelm her dainty stern. At the wheel, the helmsman kept his eyes steadfastly ahead, as a glance behind at the tumbling, towering seas was tough on the nerves. As dawn broke, the wind eased slightly and Keay wasted no time in setting sail. One by one, her upper sails and flying kites were unfurled, until the little clipper was staggering along under a huge press of sail. Her captain felt that his rivals were close at hand.

The exhilaration of the race and this wild, tumbling run home had got under his skin now, and he felt he knew exactly what his vessel could stand. Eyeing the straining rig speculatively, he ordered the fore lower stunsail to be set. It was a big sail, and the hands looked at each other fearfully. Yet they turned eagerly enough to set the sail. With a quick flog and a squeal of the tackles, the stunsail was pulled home and a huge acreage of canvas cracked once and started to hurl the ship bodily forward. 'That got her where she lives,' someone murmured,

Overleaf: By evening, the Needles were in sight.

A pilot boat and her gig off South Foreland. Picking up their respective pilots vexed both Keay and MacKinnon.

and it was true. The motion of the ship had changed and she flew like a bird on the wing from wave to wave, skipping across the smoking seas. No longer wood and canvas, a thing alive.

In the early hours of 5 September the *Ariel* was racing up the English Channel. In the hours before dawn, the red light of another ship was made out holding the same course as theirs. John Keay stared intently at this pinpoint of light as it dipped and rose, sometimes glowing in a smother of swell. He said but one word to his mate: '*Taeping*.' He had no particular reason to make this assumption, but he felt in his gut that it would be her. As dawn broke, the mysterious racer revealed herself to be MacKinnon's flyer. After all those ocean miles, not more than a couple separated the pair. They had left on the same tide and it looked like they would arrive on the same tide.

The *Ariel* had a slight lead and every possible flying kite was put out to maintain it. All day the two vessels sped up the English coastline,

running at 14 knots and more. A more beautiful sight can hardly be imagined as these two perfect ships leant purposefully into the seas that bright September day, tearing past all other shipping as if it were at a standstill. The glamour of the pair was unmistakeable, sails taut and deliberate. Their glowing curves silhouetted against the clear blue sky. Their low sleek hulls glistened and foam flecked in the clear September sun. Untouchable and perfectly matched.

What neither skipper realised was that while they were running their desperate race along the English coast, the *Serica* was racing along the French side of the Channel, barely more than a couple of hours behind. Innes, whose clipper had lagged for much of the race, had made a wonderful run up the Atlantic and was within touching distance of victory. By nightfall, the *Ariel* and *Taeping* were off the Isle of Wight and already Keay was pondering how to maintain his lead and pick up his pilot off Dungeness.

154

The fogs of the London River were a stark contrast to the soft haze of the Min River.

The *Lahloo*, built by Robert Steele, was an enlarged version of the *Taeping* and just as beautiful. She lies in the Thames and there is a tug secured to her starboard side in order to tow her alongside the dock for unloading.

GREAT RACE

OF THE

TEA SHIPS,

WITH THE FIRST

NEW SEASON'S TEAS.

PRICE OF TEAS REDUCED.

THE "Taeping," "Ariel," "Fiery Cross," and "Serica" have arrived, with others in close pursuit, with something like **FORTY-FIVE MILLION POUNDS OF NEW TEA** on board—half a year's consumption for the **United Kingdom.** This enormous weight coming suddenly into the London Docks, Shippers are compelled to submit to **MUCH LOWER PRICES**, in order to make sales.

We are thus enabled to make a Reduction of FOURPENCE in the pound.

4/0 down to - - 3/8
3/8 „ - - 3/4
3/4 „ - - 3/0

And so on downwards.

We may add the above Ships have brought a few lots of most unusual fine quality.

Reduction takes place on Friday the 21st inst.

135, OXFORD STREET;
57, STRETFORD ROAD; and
171, STRETFORD ROAD—
"Great Northern."

BURGON & CO.,
TEA MERCHANTS.

This notice eloquently attests to the disaster created by the four leading clippers arriving almost simultaneously.

The vessels raced on through the night and at 3 am were burning blue lights in preparation for picking up their pilots. Keay, aboard the *Ariel*, shortened sail. To the horror of all aboard, he and his crew saw that the *Taeping* seemed to have little intention of doing the same, threatening to overtake and steal the *Ariel*'s pilot from under her bows. Tales of the *Serica*'s misfortune the previous year when the *Fiery Cross* had stolen in ahead flooded back to Keay. He determined to put a stop to MacKinnon. Taking a huge risk, he cut across the *Taeping*'s bow at close quarters.

It was dangerous to the point of recklessness, but a lot rested on the result of the race and Keay also knew that MacKinnon was a man of impeccable common sense. Thankfully, the *Taeping*'s skipper backed down and promptly shortened sail. At 5:55 am the *Ariel* rounded to close to one of a pair of pilot cutters which had sped out from Dungeness to intercept the clippers. Captain Keay was saluted as the first ship from China, but he was in no mood to celebrate. 'Yes, and what is that to the westward?', he replied, 'We have not room to boast yet.'

There was a good deal of money riding on this result and neither skipper felt the race was at an end. Not until the *Ariel* was secured to the dock could Keay be certain of victory – provided that another clipper hadn't already got in ahead. As the vessels continued up the coast, the race was closer than ever and it wasn't until dawn that they started to make preparations for towing up the Thames Estuary.

Here, the *Taeping* was fortunate and picked up a far superior tug to the *Ariel*. Keay, however, consoled his crew as both vessels would have to await the tide at Gravesend to get into London Docks. If needs be, he would hire a second tug for the final lap. It was only at Gravesend that both skippers relaxed, receiving telegraphs from their respective owners stating that they were the leading boats and that because the race was a dead heat, the premium would be split between the two vessels. In the end, the *Taeping* arrived 20 minutes earlier than her rival and MacKinnon could satisfy himself with the knowledge that he was the ultimate victor.

The race was over and the most remarkable draw had been achieved. Yet the drama continued to unfold. An hour after the *Ariel* was warped alongside the East India Dock, word spread about that the *Serica* was towing up to the West India Dock. Sailors crowded the dock gate to watch her pass by. It was remarkable: the three ships that had departed Foochow on the same tide had arrived in London within an hour and 20 minutes of each other. All had made the passage in 99 days – the quickest voyage made with the new season's tea to date.

The question on Innes' lips as he stepped ashore was whether the *Fiery Cross* had arrived and his satisfaction at discovering he had beaten his exasperating foe mollified his disappointment at losing out on the premium for being the first ship home. Robinson's *Fiery Cross* had been unfortunate with her winds in the mouth of the Channel and arrived 24 hours or so behind her rivals, with the *Taitsing* a day further back. Both were 101 days out and, in normal circumstances, they would have won the race at a canter. This year had been different, but Robinson's disgust at being beaten in this manner was hard to conceal. Next year, he swore, he would avenge this defeat.

The biggest losers of all in the race turned out to be the tea importers, for the arrival of five vessels in such rapid succession caused a glut on the market and led to a dramatic crash in market prices.

Victory was also bittersweet for MacKinnon; he died the following year, outward bound on the *Taeping*. His death was believed to be due to an internal injury sustained while heroically rescuing the Tiree ferry as he travelled home to a hero's welcome. Meanwhile, Innes, on arrival in London, was said to be so physically and mentally drained from the strain of racing that he could barely bring a cup of tea to his lips because he shook so.

As for the crews, they would soon be ready for the next round of racing; in the meantime they took leave of the beautiful ships with the old shanty ringing in their ears:

> I thought I heard the Old Man say:
> Leave her, Johnny, leave her.
> For the voyage is done and the winds don't blow
> And it's time for us to leave her.

CHAPTER SEVEN

THE *SIR LANCELOT* DEFIES THE ODDS

The Bay of Biscay in mid-December is a lonely place to be. Gale after gale sweeps over this uncompromising stretch until great icy whitecaps stir and boil the grey water. Huge rollers, carrying with them the whole rage of the wintry North Atlantic, gather at the mouth of Biscay where they seem to mass in sullen fury, before racing on and hurling themselves on the jagged fangs of the French coast. Anyone unfortunate enough to have been out here on the afternoon of 13 December 1866 would have perceived the shadowy form of a clipper ship beating through the maelstrom on her way to China. Her rain-sodden sails were almost black in the shadowy evening light and her dark hull was sometimes almost completely obscured by spume as she sliced through the water into the teeth of the south-west gale.

Every now and again the clipper would be enveloped in a sleety squall, only to emerge unbowed a few minutes later, water streaming white from her scuppers as she continued her headlong progress with grace and purpose. The mysterious ship was the *Sir Lancelot*, bound for China under the command of the redoubtable Captain Richard Robinson.

If you were able to inspect the clipper more closely, you would have perceived, in the midst of this magnificently bleak scene, a tiny pinprick of light radiating from the deckhouse. Smoke emanated from a chimney as the stove did its work within. If you had looked through the brass porthole, you would have seen the men of the port watch inside, desperately trying to get some rest

With rain-darkened sails, an unknown clipper races down the Channel.

after several exhausting days of beating down the English Channel. However, sleep was hard to come by as the men rolled and cursed in their bunks. They had been ashore too long and were as yet unused to the rhythm of the ship. They had not long left the *Sir Lancelot*'s pitching deck after being called upon to help clew up her foresail and mainsail and knew they needed some rest before coming back on duty.

The French coastline had just been blotted out by a filthy-looking squall and all knew there was trouble ahead. The rigging thrummed in the rising gale and experienced crew members sensed, even as they drowsed, that conditions were worsening. On deck they could hear the impatient tread of the skipper and the yell of orders above the din of flogging canvas. The very fabric of the clipper shuddered as she slammed into the big waves, throwing up great smothers of spray as she beat away from the treacherous coast on her way to freedom.

At 4 pm the port watch returned on deck. It was early December and night had already swallowed the clipper. The occasional star shone out, cold and remote through tattered clouds. Astern, the light of Ushant and the savage coastline of Brittany were rapidly receding. The ship was wild and beautiful

as she surged along. The crisp air was charged with salt and keen as an ice-cold blade against the skin. Up on the poop, Captain Robinson surveyed his ship, an excitable gleam in his eye. He was in his element here, free from the shackles and drudgery of shore life. He paused to examine the ever swinging compass, but remained still only for a moment, then he leapt forward again, issuing a volley of orders.

In the gloom, he had spotted an approaching squall and all turned to in order to get the clipper snugged down. As the squall closed in, visibility dropped dramatically and the wind howled balefully in the rigging and rose to a crescendo of screaming until you couldn't hear yourself think. Then, above the wind, came another noise: a sound like a thousand sheets being ripped apart, accompanied by the ominous cracking of timber and rending of canvas.

Dismasted in the Bay of Biscay
In horror, the crew looked forward and perceived through the confusion that the bowsprit had snapped off short under the weight of the wind. The headsails were thrashing around wildly, hurling

A moody coastal scene with the promise of foul weather to come.

the shattered spar around in a lethal manner. The unruly, demented canvas was booming deafeningly. Almost immediately, the foremast, no longer fully supported, crashed over the side. The mainmast and most of the mizzen followed. In two minutes the trim clipper had been almost completely dismasted, the order of spars and rigging replaced by utter chaos. In the shrieking gale, the men rushed forward, armed with axes and knives, and desperately hacked away at the rigging in a frenzied attempt to cut it free, for the spars were now overboard, acting like giant battering rams against the hull.

Several hours later, the worst of the wreckage was clear. Only the mizzen lower mast was still standing and the *Sir Lancelot* was in a desperate situation. The south-west gale was driving her inexorably back to the French coast and inevitable destruction.

Dawn found the clipper 30 miles off Ushant and things were looking bleak. Yet fortune, which had been frowning upon *Sir Lancelot* for some time, offered a crumb of hope to the beleaguered vessel. To the immense relief of everyone, the wind shifted to a full-blown southerly, giving the skipper

and crew time to rig a jury mast and square away for Falmouth. Two days after the accident, on the evening of 15 December, she dropped the hook in Carrick Roads and all on board breathed a collective sigh of relief.

For Robinson, it was a serious setback. As he trod the crackling, icy cobbles of Falmouth the next day, he pondered his misfortune. That same autumn he had endured the enormous disappointment of losing out in the 1866 China race, so he had been delighted when James MacCunn, owner of the *Sir Lancelot*, had asked him to take charge of his newest clipper. She was a sister ship to the *Ariel* and Robinson saw in her the extra speed he required to regain his dominance in the China run. Now she was set for a heavy delay and there was a real danger she would miss the China race completely.

For James MacCunn, the *Sir Lancelot*'s owner, the unscheduled arrival of his ship in Cornwall was greeted with mixed feelings. Mainly he was relieved that his enterprising new skipper had saved the vessel, but he was also aware of the logistical nightmare in trying to re-rig her. All through December the shipwrights and riggers worked like fury to get the ship ready for sea. The hull needed

The *Sir Lancelot* dismasted and drifting helplessly into the Bay of Biscay.

The wool clipper *Loch Vennachar* suffered an identical dismasting to the *Sir Lancelot* in 1892. At the time she was in the Southern Ocean and compelled to divert to Mauritius. Note the jury rig on the foremast.

The *Sir Lancelot* at anchor. Her boats were painted green as depicted in this picture. This was a tradition Robinson had taken from his early days sailing the Brocklebank Line.

to be repaired after the battering it had received from the spars, while new masts were brought in and lowered into place.

The re-rigging was carried out by a group of riggers that MacCunn had to bring in from Liverpool, as there were simply not enough local experts to carry out the job quickly. The workforce toiled night and day through the blistering cold of one of the hardest winters in 30 years. By night, huge tar barrels were lit and the riggers worked on by the light and roaring heat of the blaze. Fights broke out between the exhausted Scousers and the local Cornishmen, but work continued apace and the clipper was once again ready for sea by 31 January.

Leaving the blistering cold behind, the *Sir Lancelot* made a good run out to China. She was late, though, and Robinson received orders to load tea at Shanghai. This was a disappointment as the tea racers would all be leaving from Foochow. Shanghai was 600 nautical miles further up the coast and this meant 600 miles further to beat down the China Sea. Robinson was effectively out of the race, and it looked like his plan to avenge his

defeat in the previous year's race would have to wait until the following season.

The race line-up

Down in Foochow, the tea shippers had chosen a new vessel as their favourite. The *Maitland* had made an extremely rapid passage out to China and was a very distinctive vessel, carrying not only skysails, but moonsails above these. Most clippers only carried a single skysail on their mainmast and this extra cloud of canvas gave the *Maitland* a striking appearance. It had clearly impressed the shippers and after towing out of the Min River, she had stretched away to the open sea with her moonsails set. The old rivals *Serica* and *Taeping* were next. The biggest threat, the *Ariel*, did not get away until 13 June, a full 12 days behind the *Maitland*, but Captain John Keay had faith in his ship.

Meanwhile, up in Shanghai, the thoroughbred *Sir Lancelot* was surrounded by has-beens and also-

Overleaf: Carrick Roads, Falmouth, was the ideal shelter for the crippled *Sir Lancelot*.

163

rans. She departed on 15 June in company with the *John R Worcester* and the *Challenger*, which were hastily dropped below the horizon. Despite his substantial handicap, Robinson still believed that he could win the race. His only real hope was his own incredible ability as a skipper. It was this that had kept him at the front of the field for so long. The *Fiery Cross*, his previous command, was actually a smaller version of the supposed also-ran *John R Worcester*. The only difference was her captain and many believed that a hard-driving, diligent skipper like Robinson (or Keay of the *Ariel*) added an extra half a knot of speed over the course of the run from China to England.

Opposite: A chart of the China Sea, illustrating the intricate pattern of islands and reefs. On her 1867 voyage, the *Sir Lancelot* took the longer route marked via the Ombai Strait between Timor and Java. The route marked through the Sunda Strait is the track taken by *Sir Lancelot*'s rival *Thermopylae* in 1869. As can be seen, her captain initially shaped a course east for the Ombai Strait, but the wind switched and he headed back west, then south to Anjer (see page 179).

Captain Richard Robinson, painted in his prime.

Below: The *Maitland*'s sail plan brings home what a remarkable cloud of canvas a clipper carried. She was the only tea clipper to carry tiny moonsails above the skysails at the very top of her masts.

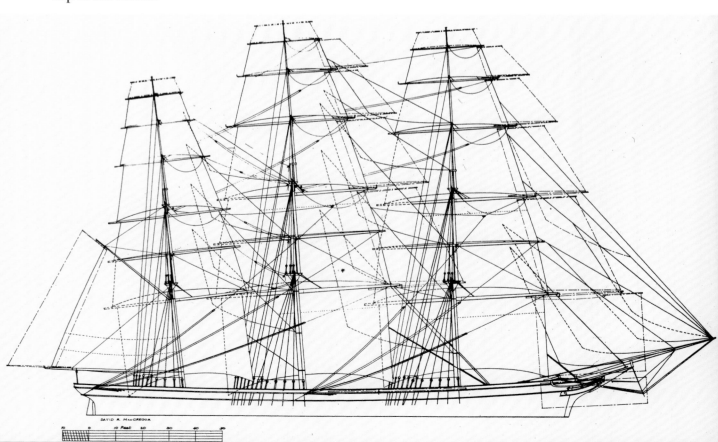

DAVID R. MacGREGOR

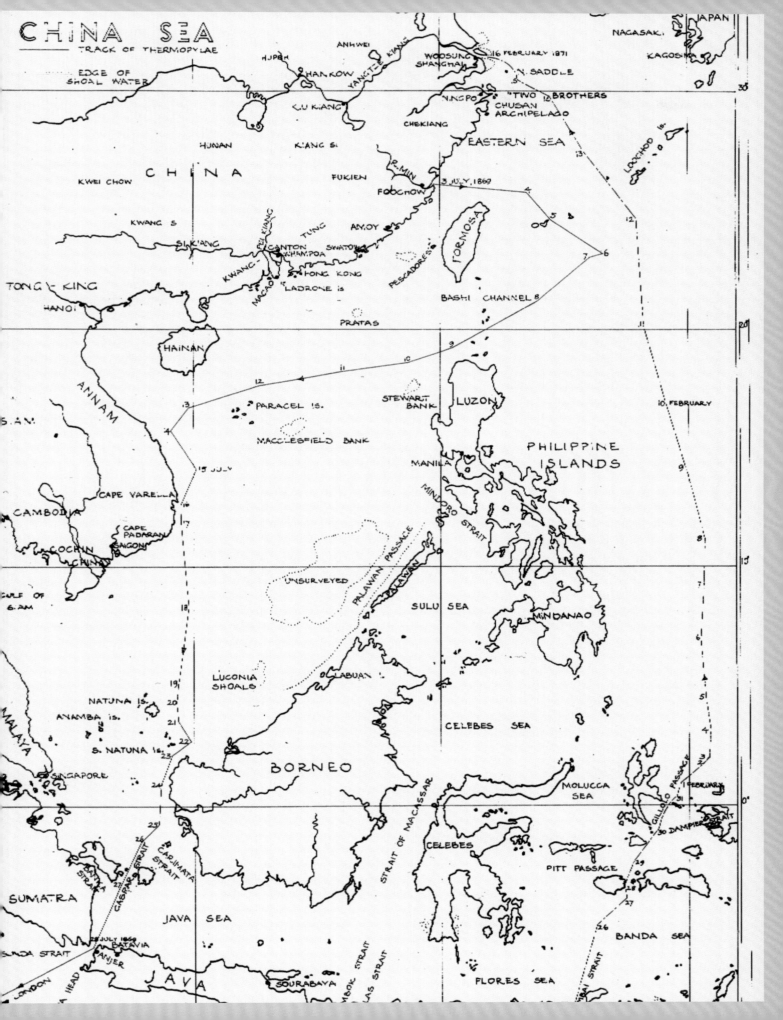

A clipper ship on the wind under a press of sail. This looks to be an example of a 'doctored' photograph, as the ship seems to be heeling over in a somewhat exaggerated manner.

'Go ahead' Robinson

Robinson was a Cumbrian who had served his apprenticeship in the Whitehaven-owned Brocklebank Line. He had quickly come to their attention as a smart but 'somewhat fiery' officer and had gained command of the *Veronica*, a China trader not noted for her speed.

His passage home in her was impressive, however, and he was approached by Chaloner, owner of the *Fiery Cross*, to command the crack clipper. This was Robinson's opportunity and he did not disappoint, winning three of the next four season's races. These performances earned him the nickname 'go ahead' Robinson as, even on land, he always seemed to be in an incredible hurry. This led to an incident often spoken of in jest amongst clipper crews. Robinson was taking a stroll through Foochow with some of his fellow skippers. He was bedecked in a magnificent suit of pale silk. As always, he was in a burning hurry and, on entering a narrow alleyway, he barged ahead of the group to a chorus of irritated cries. At this moment, one of the occupants of the boarding houses that lined the narrow street opted to empty the contents of a chamber pot out of the window all over Robinson's magnificent suit. He beat a hasty and undignified retreat back to his vessel, paying a high price on this occasion for his impatience.

Yet it was this burning urgency of spirit that ensured he was a man who lived to drive a ship hard. His energy meant that he had the will to keep pushing onward day and night. He also enjoyed the challenge of navigating the China Sea. A narrow, reef-studded passage was a thrill to him rather than something intimidating. Perhaps his most striking philosophy was his strong dislike for bracing the yards sharp up and beating into the wind. Robinson wasn't afraid to add a few more miles to a voyage as long as he could keep his vessel moving full and by through the water.

As the *Sir Lancelot* ran down the China Sea, this philosophy dictated that he took a much longer course than usual. Generally vessels made for the Sunda Strait, to the west, but on this occasion the breeze held for the Ombai Strait, over 1,000 nautical miles further east. The route was longer, but the *Sir Lancelot* was running free before the wind and that was all Robinson cared for.

The *Sir Lancelot* catches up

Despite the substantial extra mileage, the *Sir Lancelot* made a quick passage out of the China Sea and hopes were up; perhaps it was going to be possible to win the race after all. The clipper stormed out into the Indian Ocean and her ever hustling skipper let the boat fly before the breeze

168

in no uncertain style. Day after day she raced across a glittering azure sea, her bow wave hissing by with the power of a fire hydrant, throwing up great billowing clouds of white water with every thrust of the ship, her sails curved with the wind, purposeful and beautiful. The south-east trades seemed to acknowledge the urgency of the situation and hurried her along her way.

Off the Cape of Good Hope, she ran into one of her rivals, the *Flying Spur*, which had left Foochow six days before the *Sir Lancelot*'s departure from Shanghai. As the *Sir Lancelot* approached, Frederick Paton, midshipman aboard the *Flying Spur*, rubbed his eyes in disbelief at what he saw. He described the scene thus: 'It was a stormy day and the wind was a "dead muzzier" [on the nose]; *Flying Spur* was carrying what we considered to be a heavy press of sail, *viz:* whole topsails and courses with outer jib, whilst other ships in company were

close reefed. But *Sir Lancelot*, coming up on the opposite tack so as to cross the other's bow, was actually carrying three topgallant sails and flying jib.

'We looked at the approaching clipper with amazement, for the amount of canvas *Sir Lancelot* was staggering under was tremendous considering the wind. Indeed such cracking on would not have been possible but that she had the run of the sea abaft the beam, whereas *Flying Spur* and the ships on the other tack had it before the beam. As the two clippers converged on each other, they began signalling, and this nearly led to disaster on the *Sir Lancelot*, for just as she was athwart the hawse of the *Flying Spur*, her helmsman, paying more attention to the latter's signal halliards than to his own steering, allowed his ship to come up in the wind and get aback.

'In a moment the *Sir Lancelot* was heeling over

The *Sir Lancelot*'s bow.

The *Sir Lancelot* anchored at the Pagoda anchorage. The iron clipper *Blackadder* is to the left.

and getting stern-way – within an ace of being dismasted. We were so close to the clipper that we saw the watch below come flying on deck in their shirt tails. *Sir Lancelot*'s crew were as smart as paint in whipping the sail off her, and the clipper brought her spars to windward and stood up, but it was a close shave. As things calmed down, we saw Captain Robinson spring upon his careless helmsman, knock him down and jump on him.'

Several days later, the *Sir Lancelot* was racing up to St Helena when a clipper under a huge press of canvas was sighted ahead. This proved to be the shippers' favourite, the *Maitland*, and as Robinson's vessel closed with her rival, it was evident she was hanging out every single one of her many flying kites, including her much-vaunted moonsails. It was no use, though: the *Sir Lancelot* was too much for her. As his vessel forged ahead, Robinson signalled: 'Goodbye, I shall be forced to leave you if you cannot set more sail.' The crew loved him for that. They were utterly triumphant now. The *Sir Lancelot* seemed invincible and the

men were jubilant and exhilarated. The weeks of demand and toil paid off in a few perfect hours.

On she raced; Robinson's old rival the *Serica* was passed in the night. He didn't know it, but he was really only racing the *Ariel*. The rest of the pack had fallen behind, blown away both by the miracle of these two vessels and the unparalleled skill of their commanders. The *Ariel* was also flying. She had also passed the *Serica* and then overhauled the *Fiery Cross* in the run up the Atlantic, although she had only dropped the veteran racer after an epic tussle. She now seemed on course for victory, having reached Bishop Rock on 20 September 1867.

The *Sir Lancelot* had actually sighted land on 19 September, a full day before the *Ariel*, but that land was Mizen Head, Ireland. Robinson's desire to keep his ship flying was leading to unusual results. As dawn broke, there was a deputation among the excited crew; they were 96 days out of Shanghai, a passage never before approached, yet all was utter confusion: 'Where the hell is the old man taking us?' they muttered, utterly bemused. The usual landfall would have been the Lizard peninsula on the Cornish coast.

On 20 September the *Sir Lancelot* was beating up between Bishop Rock and Seven Stones, a most unorthodox piece of navigation for a big ship, but it was a piece of daring that paid off. She turned the corner into the English Channel and romped up before a fair south-westerly, docking in 99 days. The *Ariel*, arriving in the chops of the Channel a couple of hours later, found the breeze had slackened away to nothing and was ultimately vanquished. The China race was won against all the odds and Robinson was confirmed as the captain to beat above all others.

A new rival

Where do you go from there? Robinson had won the race more than any other, yet he continued to push on. In 1868, he made the trip in 98 days, but was narrowly beaten by his great rival Captain Innes, who had quit the *Serica* and was in charge of a beautiful new clipper, the *Spindrift*. In 1869, however, he produced a performance that truly set him apart from the rest.

The *Sir Lancelot* was once again late to reach Foochow, and when she arrived, Robinson and his crew found that the focus was firmly on another ship, soon to be a legend in fo'c'sles the world over: the *Thermopylae*. The name of this Aberdeen-built clipper had already been mentioned along the coast, while the *Sir Lancelot* had undertaken a gruelling

A photograph of the Pagoda anchorage in 1869. At the far left is the *Ariel* and beside her lies the *Thermopylae*. In the middle of the anchorage, the *Serica* is drying her sails and the *Lahloo* is to the right, seen stern on.

A fine image of the *Thermopylae* at anchor. This is an example of a photograph that has been painted over.

series of intermediate voyages in the China Sea. After racing out to Hong Kong, the *Sir Lancelot* had fitted in four passages laden with rice between Saigon, Bangkok, Hong Kong and Yokohama. This was exhausting work, with the crew alternately sweltering in the unbearable heat of these stifling ports and then being driven like fury by their demented skipper whenever they escaped the cloying heat of the land. By June, they were pretty much done in and were hugely relieved when the last of the rice was discharged in Yokohama and the ship raced to Foochow to join the tea fleet.

The *Sir Lancelot* reached Foochow on the morning of 20 June 1869 and spent the day working her way up the tortuous narrows of the Min River. She made the tranquil waters of the Pagoda anchorage with the last of the evening light. The *Sir Lancelot* shattered the peace as her anchors were dropped with a roar and a shower of sparks. Silence returned and the exhausted crew made out the shadows of their rival vessels in the last glow of evening. Tall spars silhouetted charcoal black against the dark hills and shimmering moon-kissed water, anchor lights already twinkling in the gloom. The crew tumbled gratefully into their bunks for some well-earned rest. Shortly thereafter only the steadfast tread of the watchman could be heard aboard.

Being selected for anchor watch after a demanding passage was definitely a case of drawing the short straw. On this night, however, with the cool night air above and water gently murmuring below, there was some rest and repose for the luckless man tasked with patrolling the deck. Only the incessant tropical showers interrupted the peace. As dawn approached, the man on watch was also treated to a truly magical sight. The first rains of the monsoon season had rendered the Pagoda anchorage almost unbearably humid, and steams and mists lay soft on the steep valley sides of the Min Gorge and poured across the glassy waters of the anchorage where the clipper fleet lay.

The *Salamis* was built in 1875 as an iron version of the *Thermopylae*, but was ten feet longer than her composite sister. She was also extremely fast and proved to be the quickest iron ship in the Australian wool trade.

Thermopylae lying at the Pagoda anchorage awaiting her cargo of tea.

Opposite top: The Pearl River, Macao. One of the many stopovers which held up the *Sir Lancelot* during her lengthy spell of intermediate passages in 1869.

Opposite bottom: Clippers and sampans in a Chinese anchorage.

Above top: The *Thermopylae* seemed utterly invincible as she raced down the Indian Ocean and the *Leander* was no match for her.

Above bottom: The *Sir Lancelot* running down the China Sea under a press of sail.

The *Thermopylae* running well in the Indian Ocean.

As the first glow of dawn illuminated the scene, the drowsy watchman stirred, tapped out his pipe on the rail and peered through the mists as the beautiful ships were slowly revealed. They were eyed with pleasure by the old seaman and counted off like old friends. The elegant *Spindrift*, winner of the previous year's race, lay above them; the *Taeping*, *Ariel*, *Lahloo*, *Serica* and *Leander* were nearby. Yet there was one newcomer that gave pause; a stranger among friends, her hull was not black like the others, but a rich dark green. The watchman strained to make out her name and, lit by the first rays of dawn, the letters glinted gold: *Thermopylae*.

and sailed out to Melbourne under the command of Robert Kemball in the autumn of 1868, breaking the record to the port with a passage of 60 days. She had then sailed across to Shanghai from Sydney and promptly broken that record too, with a 28-day run. Now she had come to Foochow to put the cream of the China tea clippers to the sword.

All lauded her achievements, but she had already caused quite a stir in Foochow among the senior skippers of the tea fleet. On her main mast, the *Thermopylae* was proudly displaying a gilt cockerel at her masthead, emblazoned with the motto 'While I live, I'll crow', spelling out all too clearly to the gathered fleet that the *Thermopylae* was their superior. To the Victorian seafarers, this unseemly display of bragging was too much. After all, the new ship had yet to prove herself on the China run.

Robert Kemball and his officers found themselves rather subtly being given the cold shoulder. In the sweltering heat of the day, as the clippers were loaded with teas by the Chinese stevedores, the skippers would retire to the shade of huge awnings rigged over the decks of the clippers or recline in cane chairs on the cool verandahs of the club house. As they unwound, they cogitated on the new arrival and her masthead adornment. It was difficult not to fume at the gall of this newcomer. Crews were also simmering with resentment as they laboured in the sticky heat, and there was much talk of how to bring the cocksure newcomer down a peg or two.

A couple of nights later, a group of seamen aboard the *Taeping* decided to take action. One daring sailor opted to swim across to the newcomer and, sneaking aboard, stole the cockerel and smuggled it back to his own ship. Uproar ensued the following day and Kemball turned on his fellow skippers, accusing them of being in on the scheme. True or not, no one owned up and the cockerel was not restored to the *Thermopylae*'s masthead until a replacement was supplied on her return to London. It is fair to say that emotions were running high as the clippers were loaded with tea.

The bad blood must have made Kemball all the more determined to beat the tea fleet home. Nevertheless, the *Thermopylae* was not the first vessel away. The shippers still favoured the *Ariel*, despite the fact that John Keay, her skipper since

As the sun burnt through and the sampans started to go about their daily work, Captain Robinson was rowed ashore and made inquiries about the strange new vessel. He didn't have to wait long to find out more as the port was abuzz with talk of the newcomer. She had been launched in Aberdeen earlier in the year for the White Star Line

177

Two different views of the *Spindrift*, a very fast and beautiful vessel. She was commanded by Robinson's old rival George Innes and he was completely duped by Robinson during their encounter off the Cape of Good Hope in 1869. The *Spindrift* was lost later that year in the English Channel due to a negligent pilot. The loss of the vessel was said to have led to have broken the heart of her owner, James Findlay.

Men working in the rigging. On a clipper ship, the constant shifting and tweaking of sails meant endless work and many older sailors avoided clipper ships for this reason.

1866, had left her the year before. It was the *Ariel*, followed by the *Leander* and the *Lahloo*, that were first away and first to be towed through the steep gorge of the treacherous Mingan Pass. The *Thermopylae* left a few days later, banners streaming. A puff of smoke and the boom of her cannon echoed around the Pagoda anchorage to announce her departure. Imagine the frustration aboard the *Sir Lancelot*, still only partially loaded, as her new rival slipped by. Yet loading had to continue and it was some 12 days before she finally got away.

Against the *Thermopylae*

Skimming down the China Seas, the *Thermopylae* gradually picked off vessels that had left ahead of her. The *Ariel*'s new skipper was not as confident in these treacherous waters and was overhauled before she reached the Sunda Strait, gateway to the Indian Ocean. Kemball had made it in 25 days; a good time, but not a record. Two weeks behind, Robinson was pushing the *Sir Lancelot* with all of

his usual tenacity, using every last ounce of guile to close the gap on his rival; this was a race against the clock and every minute counted. This year of all years, Robinson had reason to race for home; he knew that his wife was pregnant with their first child, the due date some two or three months away. He was distracted with worry about her and the sooner he got home, the better. He drove his vessel with real intent. The *Sir Lancelot* reached the Sunda Strait in 21 days, a truly remarkable run.

Running down to Mauritius, the *Thermopylae* started to realise her potential, skipping between the sparkling waves joyously, completely at one with the wind. It was at this point that the *Leander* was overhauled. This beautiful clipper was passed at close quarters, and her mate described the encounter thus: '*Thermopylae* closed on us rapidly and bore down on us, the most magnificent picture of a ship, she truly walked the waters like a thing of life. We could do nothing but cheer as that damned Scotsman passed us by.'

By the time the Cape of Good Hope had been

The *Thermopylae* at rest.

rounded, it was clear that the *Thermopylae* was making a phenomenal run and any concerns Kemball may have had about his rivals were being blown asunder by his vessel's exhilarating speed. The friction at the Pagoda anchorage was forgotten. What did he care, when his ship leapt from wave to wave, her every fibre trembling from the power of the wind in her sails. He was going for a third consecutive record and the miracle of his ship was driving him inexorably to a place in the history books. His crew were jubilant, too; they were racing for home and history. So enthused were they by their ship's speed that they even spread their jackets in the rigging to help her along.

Behind them, the *Sir Lancelot* continued to make good time. Robinson never slept and if any of the mates thought about slacking off, he was on to them in a moment. He had perfected the delicate balancing act of pushing hard enough to get maximum speed out of the boat while not breaking anything. To him it was a fine art. Sleep

could wait until the passage was at an end. Yet fatigue was making him behave oddly. Off the Cape of Good Hope, the *Sir Lancelot* caught up with the *Spindrift*, under the command of Robinson's oldest rival, Innes. Many times over the years he had tormented his fellow skipper and once again he couldn't resist it.

Under normal circumstances, a passing vessel would run alongside and signal her name, yet Robinson opted to stand off and signal the name of an entirely different ship, the *City of Dunedin*. Poor Innes was completely fooled and the *Sir Lancelot* slid past and disappeared over the horizon. Why he did this to his old adversary, no one knows, but it is possible that he didn't want to end up in a duel with the formidable *Spindrift*, for Innes would have chased very hard, had he realised this was one of his rivals.

Up the Atlantic, only the *Thermopylae* and the *Sir Lancelot* were in the race, the rest of the fleet left far behind. Robinson was never going to be able to claw back his 12-day handicap, so the race winner was going to be the skipper who made the fastest time. Once the *Thermopylae* reached the Azores, the crew knew they were witnessing something remarkable. For the first time there was talk of a third consecutive record. Imagine the glory of it; a round-the-world voyage setting a new record time on each consecutive passage. It was unheard of, yet all on board knew that it was possible if the wind just held.

The previous record for the passage made against the south-west monsoon had been set the year before by the *Spindrift*, which had made it home in 97 days. Yet, on a crisp October day, the *Thermopylae* came slashing up the English Channel, signalling the Lizard light off the Cornish coast on her 90th day out. On being boarded by her pilot, Kemball welcomed him aboard heartily and then urged him to inspect the clipper's lee rail. 'You see that rail?' he said. 'That's the first time it has been out of the water since we left China.' She then raced up the Channel to dock on her 91st day out, a phenomenal record.

Imagine cutting six days off the fastest time ever previously made. Truly she had earned her gilded cockerel, and Kemball rightly basked in the plaudits of this incredible achievement. As the dark green clipper was hauled into East India Dock, a welcome committee was already waiting, champagne in hand, to greet the crew. Kemball was the toast of the shipping world, and the celebrations and champagne receptions went on for a full week.

Robinson's final record

On the morning of 10 October, festivities had died down. The last chests of tea had been removed from the *Thermopylae*'s hold and the ship lay silent and at peace. Yet Captain Kemball was pensive; word had been passed to him that the *Sir Lancelot* had signalled her number off the Lizard lighthouse and was proceeding up the Channel. She was just 85 days out. On board the *Sir Lancelot*, neither skipper nor crew could quite believe the time they had made and they could barely imagine that they were still racing the *Thermopylae* for the record. This was just as well, for light winds meant it took them a further four days to make it to London – making her time a still astonishing 89 days.

The port of London during the age of sail. Clipper ships usually unloaded in East India or West India docks.

The Suez Canal was opened in 1869. It dealt the China tea clipper fleet a crippling blow.

Below and opposite: Two examples of the kind of racing steamers that were rendering the clipper ships redundant as soon as the Suez Canal opened. Many captains, including Richard Robinson, switched to steam simply because the money was far better, but the level of skill required was far lower.

The pride of the tea fleet had been maintained, and you can only imagine the chagrin of Kemball as the *Sir Lancelot* was hauled alongside East India Dock, bedecked with flags. The *Thermopylae* had held the China record for all of 12 days. Yet there was to be no champagne for the hard-pressed skipper of the *Sir Lancelot*, for even before he stepped ashore Robinson discovered that his wife, Mary, had died in childbirth. Heartbroken, he returned home to Cumberland even as the first cases of tea were being landed from his ship and the newspapers were heralding his achievement. Every day that he had pushed the *Sir Lancelot* to the limit to get her home, he had been racing headlong towards a devastating truth that dwarfed the race itself.

Robinson never commanded a clipper again. This desperate, doomed, magnificent final race with the *Thermopylae* marked the end of an era. 1869 was the year in which the Suez Canal was built, rendering the long passage around the Cape of Good Hope redundant. Steamships, which had previously struggled to make the trip pay, were suddenly in the ascendancy and the days of the tea clippers were numbered.

By 1870, much of the zest had gone out of the racing, as it was clear that a steamship would have her teas on the market long before the first clipper. The *Sir Lancelot* made her final passage loaded with tea in 1878 and the *Thermopylae* in 1881. Neither again made the trip home in under 100 days. As for Kemball, he retained the command of the *Thermopylae* until 1879 and was made commodore of the Aberdeen White Star Line. Despite the controversy, the *Thermopylae* carried her gilded cockerel proudly at her masthead for the rest of her days.

As for Robinson, he gathered together the pieces of his life and eventually remarried. Never again, however, did he tread the decks of a clipper ship racing before the breeze. He returned to the tea trade as master of one of the new racing steamships, the SS *Lord of the Isles*. What he made of this comparatively mundane life after the demands of racing clipper ships is not known, but his exuberance and skill marked him out as the ultimate tea clipper captain and his exploits deserve to be remembered.

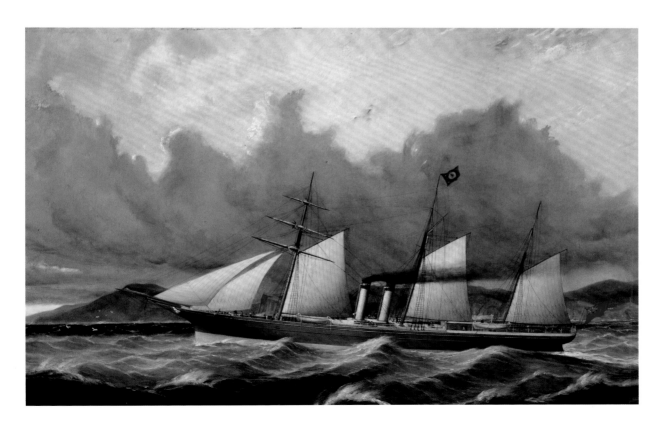

CHAPTER EIGHT

THE *CUTTY SARK'S* LONGEST VOYAGE

For three days the clipper ship *Cutty Sark* had lain hopelessly becalmed off the coast of Java, her sails limp and listless. Aboard her, the crew observed the same stretch of coastline with apathy. Every day the boat was borne by the tide up the coast a few miles, only to be deposited back in the same familiar position a few hours later. It was hot, unbearably hot. Each dawn the sun would rise refreshed after a night's rest and brutalise the ship. By midday, the heat blurred the horizon and beat down upon the deck until the pitch bubbled in its seams. The sailors cowered under the scant shade provided by the lifeless sails. Darkness brought little relief, for it simply seemed to envelop them in the cloying heat, and all hands would settle down to a night of sweating torment, accompanied by the creak of the ship and groaning of gear. Somewhere on the shoreline, a beacon would wink mockingly at them until dawn finally came.

It was the kind of sticky, humid heat that makes you gasp like a landed fish and it rendered normal shipboard work unbearable. It required a great economy of movement to ensure you didn't become irritable. Even a short walk along the deck was an exhausting chore. Yet, aboard the *Cutty Sark*, there was no effort being put into work, for her crew had refused duty. Only the afterguard of officers and apprentices were handling the clipper. Meanwhile, their captain paced the after deck in a state of utter consternation. The crew had gathered forward, congregating in any small pools of shade present.

They muttered angrily to one another about the injustice of their situation. Arthur Sankey, an

The *Cutty Sark* loading tea alongside her deadly rival, *Thermopylae.*

Left: Having refused duty, the sailors of the *Cutty Sark* had nothing to do but laze around.

Opposite: A fine action shot of the clipper *Illawarra* under sail. This vessel was an example of the later iron clippers which the *Cutty Sark* was competing within the 1870s and 1880s.

apprentice serving aboard, later recalled that there was one particular old salt who was more voluble than the rest in his complaints. He was a Dutchman and his grating voice croaked out endless tirades throughout those interminable days of calm. 'This is what comes of sailing on a Friday,' he rasped. 'The ship is doomed; did I not foretell back in Swansea that her sails would run red with blood before the voyage was out?' His pessimistic rants continued through the suffocating afternoon until finally someone told him to shut up.

This merchant of doom had indeed started with his evil prophesies the moment the clipper had left Wales. The old sailor was unquestionably half mad and he had quickly been picked out by

Above: The china tea clipper *Lahloo* ghosting along in the lightest of airs. In such conditions, the Robert Steele-designed clipper would have had the upper hand over the *Cutty Sark*.

Right: Every vessel usually had one Jonah aboard and, on this passage, Vanderdecken sapped everyone's morale.

the young apprentices aboard as a figure of fun and been given the nickname 'Vanderdecken', after the doomed captain of the *Flying Dutchman*. Yet what had seemed amusing back in Britain was far more disturbing when your boat lay in a clock calm, adjacent to a savage and unknown land, many miles from the cosy comforts of home. Much had happened since the *Cutty Sark* had left her home country and even her most sunny-natured crew member was starting to believe that the old fool's prophesies just might be true.

Back on the poop, things were becoming unbearable for Captain Wallace, who was worried sick about the situation; the intractable crew, the endless calm, the unbearable heat… He knew

The *Cutty Sark* under way in light airs.

that his nerves were shot. He hadn't slept since the clipper had departed Anjer, at the entrance to the Sunda Strait. Since then he had endured nothing but worry. His dream of commanding a fine clipper had turned into a nightmare. He paced the afterdeck with the look of a man absorbed in a puzzle that he simply couldn't fathom.

Towards 4 am on the fourth day of that seemingly endless calm, he emerged from his cabin with a new air of purpose. His face was clear and lucid for the first time in days. At the wheel, the helmsman stood rattling the almost useless spokes. Sweat poured from his brow and formed an irritating droplet on the end of his nose. The ship was ghosting along at about two knots and just about had steerage way. Wallace muttered gruffly to the helmsman to keep the course. The helmsman winced at the chiding and wrestled with the spokes. As he did so, Wallace stepped noiselessly onto the taffrail and threw himself overboard. Although the ship was hove-to immediately and a boat was lowered, the captain was gone and a group of circling sharks pointed to a grisly fate. That evening, an apocalyptic sunset filled the sky, while the stunned crew, finally mobilised by the death of their kindly skipper, held an impromptu post-mortem into his untimely demise.

How had the voyage gone so wrong? The trip had started promisingly enough. Captain Wallace was a young skipper and a generous man. He had

189

The *Cutty Sark* racing along under a heavy press of sail.

recently been appointed as captain of the *Cutty Sark* and had sailed her across from New York to London in the excellent time of 19 days. She had then headed to Swansea to load coal, with instructions to stop at Java, where she would await further orders as to her ultimate destination. At this point no one aboard could have imagined that their popular and energetic captain would end his voyage by taking his own life.

The year was 1880 and the day of the clipper as queen of the seas was long gone, but the *Cutty Sark* was still a fine vessel and a prestigious command. Wallace was a man who was doing well for himself and it helped that he was an excellent sailor and a daring skipper. The only real sign of things to come had been that the vessel had departed on a Friday, considered bad luck by superstitious sailors.

Yet the voyage had started well. The *Cutty Sark* had raced down the Atlantic neck and neck with the beautiful tea clipper *Titania*, sister to the *Ariel* and just as fast. For four days the pair had run side by side and although the days of clipper ship racing were fading fast, there was much excitement aboard both ships. The contest evoked memories of the many tea clippers that had raced this stretch of ocean before. As the two clippers danced across the waves, the older sailors aboard reminisced of the golden days and spoke of the *Ariel*, *Taeping*, *Serica* and *Spindrift*, all now buried in the deep. Only a few surviving clippers clung on in the China trade, the rest driven out by the soulless steamship. Still, here were two of the fleetest clippers running out to China. It was agreed that it was a race to the Sunda Strait and eventually the two ships parted ways on slightly different courses.

Cruel mate

While the race was on, the *Cutty Sark* was also enjoying excitement of a different kind. Although Captain Wallace was a gentle soul, the same could not be said of the mate, Smith, who liked to play the 'bucko', bullying the men about their work. Like all bullies, he liked to single out the weak and, on this voyage, his malevolence fell on a man by the name of John Francis. Although Francis was a strong black man, he was an indifferent sailor, somewhat clumsy and accident-prone. Spotting this, the mate was on to him at every opportunity, driving the poor man to distraction with never-ending racial taunts.

Eventually, Francis started to answer back and, somewhat unusually, Wallace agreed to let the two men slug it out on deck in order to settle their differences. It was a strange step to allow one of his officers to fight with a common crew member, but Wallace must have felt it was the best means to defuse the situation. After 15 minutes of savage blows, the men were parted. There was no clear victor, and this was to have fatal repercussions.

A couple of weeks later, the mate was trimming sail. Francis was supposed to let go the tack, but although the mate sang out, nothing happened. Francis was obscured by the sail, so it was impossible to tell whether he simply hadn't heard the mate or was ignoring his hated tormentor. 'Bucko' Smith headed forward to find out what the problem was. He was livid; no one ignored his orders and got off lightly, least of all Francis.

Next thing anyone heard or saw was a sharp crack and a blood-curdling cry. The mate had laid Francis out on deck with a heavy blow from a

Right: **Sailors handling sails aboard the clipper** *Loch Etive.* **It was while trimming sail aboard the** *Cutty Sark* **that trouble flared up.**

An unknown clipper at anchor.

F. Brown

handspike. Smith stated that he had gone forward and been confronted by Francis wielding the handspike and, in the ensuing scuffle, had disarmed him and laid him out cold in the process. It was unfortunate that there were no witnesses, as three days later Francis died from the injury to his head, never having regained consciousness.

The mate's hazing had already ensured that the atmosphere aboard was tense and, following the death of Francis, things became unbearable. Wallace, although a consummate sailor, had no stomach for dealing with such a matter. His instincts were to pacify and please. Yet this crisis called for the strong arm and, in this, his failings were exposed. The weight of command suddenly bore heavy on the daredevil skipper. Although Smith continued with his work, the murder had given him a bad scare and he begged Wallace to help him. Wallace didn't know what to do. He was torn between the unspoken unity of the officers and his repugnance for this murderous, cowardly bully. All the while the doom-laden croakings of old Vanderdecken in the fo'c'sle rose more volubly, grating on everyone's nerves.

The *Cutty Sark* continued to race on and she was running very well, arriving off Java 69 days out from Swansea. This was a very fast passage. Yet as she approached Anjer, on the tip of Java, there was further misfortune. As she lay becalmed in the lee of the island, the crew observed their rival, the *Titania*, ghost past to win the race. In reality, this defeat was the least of Wallace's worries.

Arriving off Anjer he found no orders awaiting his clipper. The *Cutty Sark* lay there a week, and the gloom that had descended on the ship following the death of Francis now fully enveloped the vessel. It was during this interminable week that Wallace made his fatal move. Smith had been whining to him constantly to let him escape and Wallace finally caved in. Abeam of the *Cutty Sark* lay the *Colorado*, a Yankee clipper that was short-handed. Wallace agreed to collude with his mate and allow him to escape. One evening a couple of native boats came alongside offering various trinkets, food and drink to the crew of the *Cutty Sark*. Wallace gave his men some money and allowed them to trade. As the crew indulged itself in a spot of rowdy bartering, Smith slipped over the opposite rail into a rowing boat and off to the *Colorado*. When this discovery was noted, the crew was utterly outraged that Smith had escaped justice and assured their captain that there would be a full inquiry when they finally docked. In the meantime, they refused duty.

Presently, orders came to sail for Yokohama, Japan, and the anchor was weighed by the apprentices, carpenter and sailmaker. All the while the crew lounged about in a very ugly mood until Wallace clapped four of them in irons. It was at this point that the suffocating calm descended. With nothing to do, Captain Wallace had plenty of time to stew. He saw now what a fool he had been. By allowing Smith to escape, he had brought the burden of blame squarely upon himself. He visualised the inevitable inquiry in Yokohama with utter dread. He saw himself disgraced and stripped of his ticket. While the ship lay motionless and sweltering in the cloying heat, he cursed his weakness and rash actions. There seemed to be no escape. For four days he fretted until finally all became clear to him. He stepped into the blue and out of this world.

Search for a new skipper

Now the *Cutty Sark* had no master and no mate. It was also unfortunate that her second mate was almost entirely useless. Ironically, as soon as the crisis point had been reached, a breeze filled in and the clipper finally began to make way across the oily seas. The scared second mate opted to head back to Anjer and safety. Even this was not without drama as the commanderless vessel ended up drifting backwards in a strong current past the treacherous Thwart-the-way Island. So close did she pass that her yards had to be braced up sharp to prevent them touching. All breathed a sigh of relief when the hook was finally dropped. All perhaps with one exception: the *Cutty Sark*'s owner, Jock Willis.

Jock Willis was a bluff old Scotsman and sailor of some repute. He had retired from the sea and taken to ship owning, but it did not sit well with him. He missed the sea and lived vicariously

Opposite: **The *Cutty Sark* under all plain sail.**

Overleaf: **The *Cutty Sark* and *Thermopylae* racing in 1872. The rivalry between the two endured for many decades.**

193

Above: The *Blackadder* was also owned by Jock Willis and encountered the *Cutty Sark* at anchor off Sumatra following Captain Bruce's debauch.

Left: After the *Cutty Sark* had her rudder ripped off while racing the *Thermopylae* in 1872, her captain devised this jury rudder in order to get her home.

through his ships. He clung to sail, even though it was plain to all that the race was almost run. He had launched the *Cutty Sark* in 1869, the year the Suez Canal had rendered her an anachronism. He had dreamed of the *Cutty Sark* lowering the colours of the legendary *Thermopylae*, yet so far he had been disappointed. The *Cutty Sark*, although unquestionably a very fast ship, was no match for some of the more dainty clippers in light airs. In 1872 she had raced home with tea alongside the *Thermopylae* and had seemed to gain the upper hand over her rival, only to lose her rudder in a storm off the Cape of Good Hope and limp home an honourable second.

After that, a series of indifferent skippers had led to disappointing runs in the China trade. All the while, steamers undercut the clippers. Now here was Willis' troublesome vessel in difficulty again with neither skipper nor mate. At great expense, he sent her up to Singapore under the command of a pilot. There, irony of ironies, he had arranged for her coal cargo to be shipped aboard the racing tea steamship SS *Glencoe*.

Meanwhile, a new skipper was sought. As it happened, the clipper *Halloween*, also owned by Willis, was lying up the coast in Hong Kong. Her

captain, Fowler, had on board a very irritating mate named Bruce, whom he strongly disliked. Willis sent Fowler a cable enquiring whether Bruce was suitable as skipper for the *Cutty Sark*. Fowler gleefully replied in the affirmative.

Bruce was a very different man from Wallace: short, plump and rather full of himself. Nevertheless, everyone was happy to give him a chance and welcomed a fresh start for the beleaguered ship. To the relief of all, old Vanderdecken took leave of the ship and there were no more mutterings about curses and doom. The *Cutty Sark* was ordered to Calcutta and Captain Bruce strutted the deck with great dignity as she made her departure.

All went well on the passage and Captain Bruce came across as a very righteous man, holding regular prayer meetings and preaching on the evils of drink and excess. However, off Sandheads, the entrance to the Hooghly River (off Calcutta), this mask started to slip. Bruce was a terrible coward, and landfall filled him with terror. All of his bluster and bounce fell from him as the clipper approached land. He clung to the rail, pale with terror as the *Cutty Sark* jogged along under close-reefed sails. The crew were curious at this transformation, and their curiosity and amusement doubled when the clipper finally

The *Halloween* was also owned by Jock Willis and supplied the *Cutty Sark* with her new skipper.

Melbourne in the days of sail.

Having left the China trade, the *Cutty Sark* found herself competing against larger iron clippers such as the *Thessalus*. These bigger clippers were still quick and could carry a far larger cargo than the dainty tea clippers.

Two clippers, the *Salamis* and *Loch Maree*, alongside a wharf at Melbourne.

picked up a pilot and Bruce promptly regained his pompous swagger.

Tramp of the ocean

Having been taken off the China run, the *Cutty Sark* was now a tramp of the ocean. No longer a queenly tea clipper, she had to scrabble around for cargoes with the rest of the commoners. She was over four months in Calcutta before a cargo to Sydney was secured. Most of her hands had cleared out and she was compelled to ship a group of unsavoury characters who had been lounging 'on the beach' (unemployed) at Calcutta. They were hired on the understanding they could leave in Melbourne.

The trip was a slow one, not for want of wind, but for want of drive from the skipper. The *Cutty Sark* endured the indignity of being overhauled by the *Cingalese*, a very slow vessel that had left Calcutta a week later. She came foaming by, with her crew bellowing derisively at their rival. This came about because the *Cutty Sark* was closing with the coast of Australia and Captain Bruce was once more utterly paralysed with fear, keeping the vessel dodging under low canvas for days on end.

Finally a pilot was procured and the anchor was lowered. While the clipper awaited a berth in Port Philip, Melbourne, Captain Bruce again regained his swagger, promptly ordering the crew to tar down the rigging. Given that this was the end of their passage and the men were about to be discharged, they felt they had fulfilled their duty and were disinclined to undertake such arduous work. That night, they made their feelings clear by heaving the tar barrel over the side.

The next morning, undeterred, the mate found some old pots of tar and watered them down into a horrible mess. The truculent men were then ordered up the rigging to get to work. Cursing, not quite under their breath, the crew hauled themselves aloft and set to work in a very ugly mood. All was not well, and presently a tar pot came tumbling down from the rigging and splattered on the deck, leaving a disgusting mess. Soon there was a regular hail of pots as the men made their feelings eminently clear. The long-suffering apprentices

Overleaf: **Port Jackson, the entrance to Sydney Harbour.**

199

The *Cutty Sark* loading at Circular Quay, Sydney. The *Brilliant*, a much larger clipper, is moored on the inside of her.

were still scrubbing this filth off as the ship was hauled alongside the quay.

After discharging, the clipper made her way round to Sydney, where more problems arose. There was a shortage of crew to replace the tar-throwing hooligans who had quit the ship. Bruce was compelled to hire hands at twice the going rate and was utterly furious. The *Cutty Sark* loaded coal for Shanghai in company with a number of other clippers, including the *Thermopylae* and her iron sister, *Salamis*. The race was on, but with Bruce in command there was little thrill for the contest aboard the *Cutty Sark*.

Hazing and hardship

After departing Sydney there was a new and unpleasant development. Bruce and the mate had resented hiring the highly paid Sydney hands and made a pact to run them out of the ship in Shanghai where there was plenty of cheap crew available. To this end, they indulged in a brutal regime of hazing the men as the vessel ran up to China. Very little rest

was allowed and the men were constantly being put to work on the most soul-destroying and arduous of tasks. After a miserable run up the China Seas, the vessel was berthed in Shanghai and her coal was discharged. The overpaid crew had endured enough and prepared to clear out.

Yet before they could make their departure, cholera broke out and the entire crew was sent to hospital while the vessel was fumigated. Two men died and it was three weeks before the rest could return to the beleaguered vessel. All of this was deeply frustrating to Bruce, who had thought himself shot of these expensive men. He himself had stayed ashore prior to the cholera outbreak and was in good health. He eyed the returning men with a malevolent glint and immediately set them to work cleaning out the hold, which was still full of coal dust. This was too much for the convalescing men and they promptly refused duty.

Bruce smirked, as he felt he had finally nailed the men on charges of mutiny, and reported them to a judge. Thankfully, sanity prevailed and, following

Windjammers at anchor.

an investigation, Bruce was severely censured for his inhuman behaviour and was very close to losing his precious command. He returned aboard grovelling to the men like the coward he was and, for a time, the hard-used men enjoyed a respite.

The ship was now ordered to Cebu in Manila, where she would load jute for New York. At Cebu another ugly scene ensued when the crew were plied with excessive amounts of alcohol. The mate then turned on the men and a fight broke out between the mate and one of the expensive hands. The result was that the unfortunate seaman was left to rot in a Manila jail on charges of mutiny.

The following day, the *Cutty Sark* got under way. The anchor was weighed by the men in stony silence. The crew were utterly demoralised and lived in dread of what the captain would dream up next. What Bruce did do next surprised everyone. After departing Manila, the vessel made her way back to Anjer, scene of Captain Wallace's unfortunate demise many months before. Here she anchored. There was no need for her to anchor, as her orders were to proceed to New York. Nevertheless, Bruce seemed content to tarry awhile and it soon became clear why.

Drunk in command

Shortly after arrival, a native boat had come alongside the clipper and sold the mate a quantity of the local 'fire water'. The mate invited Bruce to share this, and the pair rapidly became helplessly drunk while the crew watched, mouths agape, at their undignified capers. Once the pair had become thoroughly inebriated, the bold captain issued orders to raise the anchor. This caused utter dismay aboard, for the wind and tide had turned against them and any fool could see that it would have been prudent to wait. Yet Bruce was drunk beyond reason. Tack and tack about they went, slowly being pushed back towards Java and the labyrinth of rocks and islands within the Sunda Strait.

The mate had retired to his cabin, where he was snoring volubly, while Bruce still strutted the deck in a befuddled state. The crew begged the second mate to take over and anchor the ship in a safe spot. This he refused to do while the captain still stood. A council of war was then surreptitiously held and it was agreed that the second mate must ply Bruce with more booze until he finally collapsed. Thus, as the *Cutty Sark* stole through the China Seas, captain and second mate indulged in the most

A barque at anchor.

Opposite top: **The *Cutty Sark* under way.**

Opposite below: **The *Cutty Sark* unloading goods.**

strained carousal on the poop; the junior officer, armed with a convivial grin and a wealth of spirits, plied his hated master, who continued to strut around like some kind of demented turkey.

Meanwhile, the crew awaited on the main deck, listening with bated breath to the unfolding drama, as their safety depended on the success of the scheme. Gradually, Bruce's blathering became incomprehensible and was replaced with rhythmic breathing, punctuated by the odd hiccup. The coast was clear. Bruce was dumped unceremoniously in his cabin and the boat was ransacked in a desperate search for any more 'fire water'. Any found was rapidly thrown overboard. Next, a snug anchorage was located off Sumatra and the hook went down with a rattle and a roar. All hands turned in for some well-earned sleep.

Two days later, the *Blackadder*, another clipper of the Willis line, was running towards the Sunda Strait, also bound for New York. She was making fine time, and her captain, Frederick Moore, was surveying his ship with pride, when his gaze was arrested by the sight of a fine-looking clipper anchored off the Sumatra coast. It was an out-of-the-way sort of a place to anchor and he promptly grabbed his

telescope to get a closer look. 'Who is she, sir?' the mate asked, for he had also been intrigued. 'Why, it's the *Cutty Sark*!' Moore replied with surprise. 'But what in the name of hell is she doing there?'

He was not the only one to ask that question. Captain Bruce had finally awoken and was utterly bewildered to find his command at anchor. His last memory had been of departing Anjer for the open ocean. Now, nursing the mother of all hangovers, he tried to piece together what had happened, but continually drew a blank. He quizzed his mate… nothing; second mate… silence; crew… a few muffled guffaws, but nothing else. What the hell had happened? The *Cutty Sark* got under way and followed the *Blackadder* rather sheepishly out of the Sunda Strait and into the open ocean.

Bruce knew he was in a great deal of trouble if he couldn't find out what had happened. He would have an entire crew plus the second mate as witnesses to his incompetence and he needed to know what had happened to fabricate some lie to cover his back. Throughout the passage to New York, he sought to inveigle himself with the crew in order to find out. Yet it was all to no avail: the crew hated him like poison and no one would lift a

In the Australian trade, the *Cutty Sark* was once again pitted against her old antagonist, the *Thermopylae*. Here she is pictured to the right, awaiting the season's wool clip. The other clipper is another Aberdeen ship, the *Brilliant*.

finger to help him. The big question was whether they would finally turn against him and expose him for the incompetent, bungling hypocrite he unquestionably was.

As the clipper ran up the Atlantic, something happened that settled the matter: the ship ran out of supplies. The first sign of things to come arrived off St Helena, where the crew were put on half rations. Bruce had left Manila hopelessly short of supplies for no other reason than to save a small amount of money. By the time the equator had been crossed, rations were down to a quarter and the men were getting desperate. Again they pleaded with the second mate to take over, but he refused and told them to make the best of things. Eventually they were forced to beg supplies from HMS *Thalia*, which crossed their path near Bermuda. It must have been tough for Bruce to explain why a ship famous for her speed was short of supplies, but the

captain contrived something and the hunger pangs of the crew were finally sated.

On arrival in New York, the harassed second mate asked for his discharge and Bruce, somewhat rashly, refused. With that, the sorely tried man complained to the consul and the subsequent investigation, unsurprisingly, found in favour of the crew. Both Bruce and his sinister mate had their tickets suspended.

Wool clipper

The language that Jock Willis used on discovering that, for the second time in a little over a year, his vessel was without skipper or mate must have been positively sulphurous. Yet Willis' fortunes with the little clipper were about to change and his patience and belief in her started to pay off. At this point he switched her into the wool trade, running from London to Sydney and back every year. Here

Cutty Sark hove to off Sydney, waiting for a pilot.

The four-masted barque *Port Jackson* raced for many years on the wool run and was a fine example of the kind of large windjammers which were replacing clippers like the *Cutty Sark* and *Thermopylae*. A ship like this could carry double the cargo of the *Cutty Sark*.

Above: The *Sardomene* was built in 1882, about the time that ship owners stopped building ships with speed as a priority. Although the *Sardomene* was almost double the tonnage of the *Cutty Sark*, she would have carried a similar sail area, thus greatly reducing her speed in light winds.

Opposite: In the Australian trade, the *Cutty Sark* raced and beat much larger iron clippers such as the *Argonaut*.

Fort Macquarie, Sydney. The *Cutty Sark* was a regular in Sydney for over a decade.

The *Cutty Sark* in Sydney Harbour drying her sails.

she was pitted against much larger iron clippers designed to stand up to the rigours of running before the Roaring Forties, out past New Zealand and around the Horn to home.

This was the last refuge of the clipper, as the long ocean passage in these wild waters remained uneconomical for steamships. The race was still on here, as it was vital that ships arrived back in London in time for the March wool sales. Thus, after loading in Sydney or Melbourne, a fleet of 20 or so wool clippers would sail across the desolate waters of the Southern Ocean as they raced home with the season's wool clip.

Here, the Cutty Sark found her old rival the *Thermopylae* and, although the two vessels were smaller than their iron rivals, they soon proved to be the dominant ships in the trade. Yet it was the *Cutty Sark* that proved the faster in the run home. No vessel seemed able to touch her in the very strong winds of this desolate stretch of water. Under the shrewd command of Captain Woodget, she dominated all. The tables had been turned on the *Thermopylae*, which had always got the better of her in the China race.

In 1885, the *Thermopylae* and *Cutty Sark* were both loading wool at Circular Quay, Sydney. The pair were due to leave within a few days of each other and Woodget, observing the *Thermopylae*'s gilt cockerel, commented: 'I'll pull that damned bauble off her.'

She made the run to London in 73 days and was easily the first wool clipper home. The *Thermopylae* was second, but a full week behind. Finally Jock Willis' dream of beating the *Thermopylae* had been fulfilled. The *Cutty Sark* continued to dominate the wool fleet until the 1890s, when the hated steamships started to undercut the clippers once again.

The sailing ship was reduced to being nothing more than a functional carrier of bulk goods. Sharp lines and graceful curves were replaced by slab sides and bluff lines which screamed out functionality over beauty. Yet it is poetic that the two great clipper rivals, the *Cutty Sark* and *Thermopylae*, were both there racing side by side in the final days of the clipper age defying the drab march of progress with

their desperate flying passages. Illuminating a dull port with their beauty and grace, which one simply cannot conceive in a modern cargo vessel.

Of course, you can still enjoy the *Cutty Sark*'s graceful lines, for she survives to this day, lying in stately retirement in London. Although you can still admire her in her glass cage, the place she truly belongs is unquestionably deep down in the Roaring Forties, driving before towering grey seas while the storm roars overhead and thrums through her rigging. Here, the flying clipper had only the lonely albatross for company and it was on this desolate, desperate stretch of water that the full potential of her beauty was truly unfurled: graceful, purposeful and utterly unassailable.

EPILOGUE
Twilight

In 1908 the tea clipper *Titania* was towed to a ship breakers yard in Genoa. Older sister to the beautiful *Ariel*, in her prime this vessel had overhauled the *Thermopylae* in 1871 and beaten the *Cutty Sark* in a close race in 1878. With these triumphs behind her, the beautiful little vessel had abandoned the tea trade in the late 1870s and taken up a more humble existence as a tramp of the ocean.

In the 1880s *Titania* was purchased by the Hudson Bay Company and spent over a decade tussling with Cape Horn as she travelled between Europe and Vancouver. Her low bulwarks and open deck must have made her a real caution in the storms down south, but she fought on gamely and made some excellent passages. Yet her battling was all in vain. Her sleek little hull was too sharp to carry a full cargo and dwindling dividends persuaded her owners to sell to an Italian company. Another decade of tramping and her owners gave up and sent her to the breakers. The Italians are known as a passionate nation and they know a work of art when they see one. When the ship breakers at Genoa looked over the beautiful vessel towed into their yard, they wrung their hands in dismay. They could not bring themselves to destroy such a model of perfection and beauty. It would be like putting your foot through a Monet, taking a wrecking ball to the Sistine Chapel. *Non e proprio possibile!* So the *Titania* sailed again and two years later it was the turn of the ship breakers of Marseille to wring their hands once more when she returned to their yard. This time her perfect hull was destroyed, and with it one of the last symbols of an era where beauty and function worked as equals was gone.

Scores of tall ships were laid up for months on end toward the end of the tall ship era. Sometimes they were simply awaiting the next freight, but others were just left to rust away.

Other clippers suffered more violent fates at the hands of wind and wave. Of the early American clippers, most were water-strained wrecks by the 1860s, but the great rivals *Flying Cloud* and *Challenge* were two which survived longer than most. *Flying Cloud* was sold to James Baines' Black Ball Line in 1862 and completed several voyages out to the colonies before sliding down the ranks into the lumber trade. The badly strained ship held out until 1874 when she grounded off St John, New Brunswick. For a whole year she wallowed in the surf there a total wreck, and the following summer she was burnt for her metal fittings. Her rival *Challenge* was similarly long-lived and was still tramping the seas in 1877, owned in Sunderland and

renamed *Golden City*. Despite her long life, Bully Waterman's final command was never a lucky ship and her career was blighted with accident and misfortune. Her last owner later recalled that when he bought her he was warned off this 'confounded pickpocket' of a ship. He later admitted she never made any money for him. Her end came in 1877 when she grounded off Ushant after her steering had been damaged. Rescue attempts were futile and she became a total loss. Her first captain was far more fortunate, and for the wealthy residents of Solano County in California, Robert Waterman is not remembered as a bullying passage maker and alleged murderer, but as the wise and benevolent man who helped to found the communities of

Below: A windjammer leaving Hamburg. By 1900, British ship owners had turned their back on sail, but Germany continued to run efficiently a large fleet of tall ships right up until the outbreak of World War I. The opening of the Panama Canal in 1914 was another heavy blow, however.

The *Glory of the Seas* was the last ever clipper built by Donald McKay. Launched in 1869, she was not as sharp as his earlier clippers, but still made some extremely fast passages. The building of this great ship on spec bankrupted McKay, but she remained afloat until the 1920s, a fine epitaph to a brave era.

Fairfield and Cordelia, the latter settlement named after his wife. He died in 1884, many miles from the sea in his comfortable ranch.

Little is known of the final fate of *Neptune's Car*. After the Pattens' dramatic departure, she made a number of fine passages around Cape Horn and was sold to a shipping firm in Liverpool in the 1860s, subsequently disappearing from the registers. It is likely she was renamed and her ultimate fate remains a mystery. The demise of the *Marco Polo, Lightning, Schomberg* and their unfortunate commander has been discussed in depth, which brings us to the British tea clippers. As for the veterans of the 1866 race, both ships

and commanders suffered mixed fortunes. MacKinnon of the *Taeping* died on his following voyage as already noted, and his former command was wrecked off Ladd's Reef in the China Sea in 1871. We have previously discussed the fate of the *Ariel*, overwhelmed in the Roaring Forties and posted as 'missing' for many years. Captain Keay left her in 1869 and, after dabbling with command of a few steamships he retired and lived to a ripe old age. George Innes and *Serica* were less fortunate; Captain Innes returned to his old ship after the loss of the larger, faster *Spindrift* in 1869. In 1872 he was engaged in some typically daredevil work down the China Sea when his luck finally ran out. Getting in

The *Aristides* was built for the Aberdeen White Star Line seven years after they purchased the *Thermopylae* and became the flagship of the Line, with Captain Kemball moving from the tea clipper to the new vessel. Although a beautiful ship, she was nowhere near as fast as *Thermopylae.*

among the Paracel reefs in poor weather, the *Serica* piled up on a reef and was soon destroyed. Only one of her 23 crew survived, and Innes went down with the ship that had brought him so much fame. The *Fiery Cross* and *Taitsing* enjoyed long lives, being wrecked in 1893 and 1883 respectively. Captain Robinson of the *Fiery Cross* and *Sir Lancelot* retired to his home town of Workington in Cumbria and became a Justice of the Peace. One can imagine this well-respected pillar of the community still trod the streets with an impatient, restless step until his death in the 1890s. The *Sir Lancelot* lasted as long as her famous master and was still doing good service plying between India and Mauritius until 1895 when she finally foundered in a severe cyclone.

Barring *Titania*, the *Cutty Sark* and *Thermopylae* were the last two survivors of the tea trade and after trading blows in the wool trade, they went their separate ways. For many years *Thermopylae* worked in the lumber trade, operating out of Vancouver while the *Cutty Sark* was sold to the Portuguese and tramped the North Atlantic under the name of the *Ferreira*. It is ironic that this famous pair was reunited under the Portuguese flag in 1895, when *Thermopylae* was purchased by the Portuguese government as a training ship and renamed the *Pedro Nunes*. It was under this guise that she

Australian stevedores load bales of wool aboard a tall ship. This cargo was heavily compressed in order for it to be crammed in the hold.

perished, for in 1907, the Portuguese had no further use for her and sent her out into the Atlantic where she was given a naval funeral and torpedoed, a sad end to such a perfect little vessel. Only the *Cutty Sark* soldiered on, shuffling into obscure ports, all threadbare rigging and peeling paint until she was finally rescued and restored in 1922. I should also mention that the *City of Adelaide*, a beautiful little clipper built in Sunderland in 1864 and originally operating in the Australian trade, is the only other clipper to have survived, rotting away in a number of Clyde backwaters. Yet even as I write she is being transported from what looked to be her grave in Irvine, Scotland to Adelaide, where her preservation will take place.

Commercial sail still had a long way to go, but by 1900 twilight was setting in. The clippers were

finished and those that weren't destroyed endured the indignity of being turned into coal hulks to feed the rapacious steamships. It was the turn of the mighty four-masted barques to take their turn. These latter day tall ships had their own majesty and beauty. Some were almost double in length to the clipper ships. Studding sails and flying kites were a thing of the past and sharp lines, sleekness and speed were replaced by vessels shaped by more utilitarian needs: cargo capacity, ease of handling, practicality. Speed was often of very little import in these later vessels, which were often treated as little more than floating warehouses. It would be the dark waters of Cape Horn and the screaming wasteland of the Roaring Forties that would prove to be the final refuge of the mighty windjammers. Racing home to Europe from Australia loaded with

The wool clipper *Miltiades* anchored in Sydney Harbour. She has no cargo aboard and rides high out of the water, showing her perfect lines to good advantage.

a cargo of grain, these powerful vessels ran before the great winds of the Southern Ocean with only the lonely albatross and the relentless westerly gales for company. Even with small crews, rust-spattered decks and blistered hulls, they still had a power, grace and beauty that no mechanically driven vessel can ever hope to replicate. The final grain race took place in 1939 and the last ships were finished off by World War II. Only a handful of tall ships survive as museums or training ships. We all should feel the death of commercial sail, for with the passing of these great ships, the oceans have lost something beautiful, something that transcended mere function.

The writer Joseph Conrad served aboard *Loch Etive* and the *Torrens*, clippers that raced alongside the *Cutty Sark* and *Thermopylae* on the Australia run. He felt the loss of the great sailing ships keenly perfectly summed up the loss with great poignancy:

History repeats itself, but the special call of an art which has passed away is never reproduced. It is as utterly gone out of the world as the song of a destroyed wild bird. A modern ship does not so much make use of the sea as exploit a highway with a thudding rhythm in her progress and the regular beat of her propeller, heard afar in the night with an august and plodding sound as of the march of an inevitable future. But in a gale, the silent machinery of a sailing-ship would catch not only the power, but the wild and exulting voice of the world's soul.

APPENDIX
Principal records set by British and American clipper ships

East coast of North America to California

1851	*Flying Cloud*	New York to San Francisco	89 days
1854	*Flying Cloud*	New York to San Francisco	89 days
1861	*Andrew Jackson*	New York to San Francisco	89 days

California to east coast of North America

1853	*Comet*	San Francisco to Boston	76 days
1853	*Northern Light*	San Francisco to Boston	76 days
1853	*Sovereign of the Seas*	Honolulu to New York	82 days

China to England

In calculating any record from China to England, you have to make allowances for the seasonal monsoon. The south-west monsoon blows from May to September, while the north-east monsoon blows from October to April. This means a ship leaving during the south-west monsoon would often have to beat down the China Sea, which added many days to the passage.

One must also make allowances for vessels sailing from Shanghai as opposed to Foochow or Hong Kong. Shanghai is 600 nautical miles to the north of Foochow and this could add several days to a passage, particularly during the south-west monsoon.

Against the south-west monsoon

1869	Sir Lancelot	Foochow to London	89 days
1869	Thermopylae	Foochow to London	91 days
1871	Titania	Foochow to London	93 days
1867	Sir Lancelot	Shanghai to Mizen Head	96 days
1869	Titania	Shanghai to Deal	96 days

With the north-east monsoon

1873	Lothair	Hong Kong to Deal	88 days
1864	Taeping	Amoy to Deal	88 days
1874	Halloween	Shanghai to Start Point	89 days
1852	Witch of the Wave	Canton to Dungeness	90 days
1855	Nightingale	Shanghai to Beachy Head	91 days

England to Australia

1868	Thermopylae	London to Melbourne	63 days
1854	James Baines	London to Melbourne	64 days
1874	Thermopylae	London to Melbourne	64 days
1874	Ben Voirlich	Plymouth to Melbourne	64 days

Australia to England

1854	Lightning	Melbourne to Liverpool	63 days
1886	Cutty Sark	Sydney to Ushant	67 days
1869	Patriarch	Sydney to Ushant	68 days

Transatlantic

1854	James Baines	Boston to Rock Light	12 days
1854	Red Jacket	Sandy Hook to Bell Buoy	12 days

The tea clipper *Maitland* running before a fresh breeze. This vessel was built in Sunderland in 1865 and on her maiden voyage she ran out from Sunderland to Hong Kong in 87 days. Only the *Ariel* has bettered this passage, making the run in 83 days from London to Hong Kong in the same year.

Overleaf: A map that picks off the track of the five main protagonists in the 1866 China Tea Race showing their daily progress. Given that all of the vessels arrived within 48 hours or so of each other, it is interesting to note how frequently their courses diverged, particularly in the China Sea. The various coloured tracks denote the different vessels as follows: Black: *Ariel*. Red: *Taeping*. Blue: *Serica*. Dotted: *Fiery Cross*. Green: *Taitsing*.

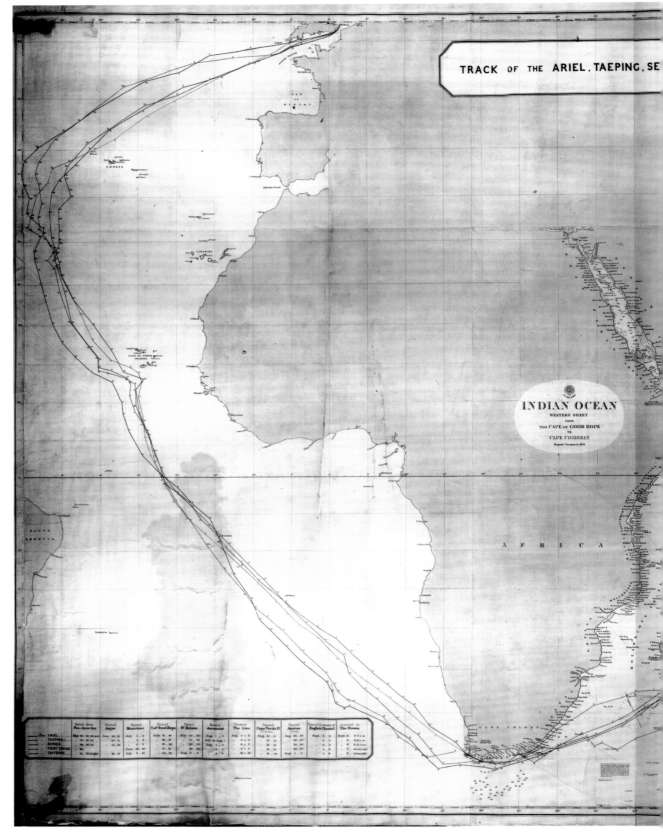

INDIAN OCEAN
WESTERN SHEET
FROM
THE CAPE OF GOOD HOPE
TO
CAPE COMORIN

Taitsing, oil on canvas, unknown Chinese artist, on loan from Mr Anthony J. Hardy

「神箭號」，油彩布本，中國佚名藝術家，由何安達先生借出。

Ship-rigged composite clipper, 190' x 31'5" x 20' 1", 815NRT, built 1865, Chas. Connell & Co, Glasgow

「神箭號」是一艘全武裝的疾速帆船，長190呎，濶31呎5吋，高20呎1吋，重815公噸。1865年由Chas. Connell & Co, Glasgow所建造。

In the Great Tea Race of 1866, under the Findlay & Longmuir house flag, the *Taitsing* (Capt. Daniel Nutsford) completed her maiden voyage. She was the last of the first five ships to leave Fuzhou for London. After 14,000 miles at sea the leading four ships arrived within 24 hours of each other, the *Taitsing* the two days later. This track chart from the United Kingdom Hydrographic Office Archive, made by a contemporary amateur enthusiast after the race, shows the daily progress of all five. The *Taitsing* sank off Nyuni Island, Zanazibar, on 20th Sept. 1883.

1866年正值茶葉貿易熱潮期間，「神箭號」懸上Findlay & Longmuir的旗幟，由船長Daniel Nutsford帶領下進行首航，她是五艘最先到倫敦作茶葉貿易船隊中最後離開福州的。經過14,000米的航程，四艘船先後抵達，每船抵達時間相差不足24小時，而「神箭號」則於兩天後才抵達。這一幅圖由英國地形測量處提供，是由一位當代業餘的海事愛好者製作，顯示出五艘船每日的進程。1883年9月20日，「神箭號」不幸於桑吉巴的紐尼對開海面沉沒。

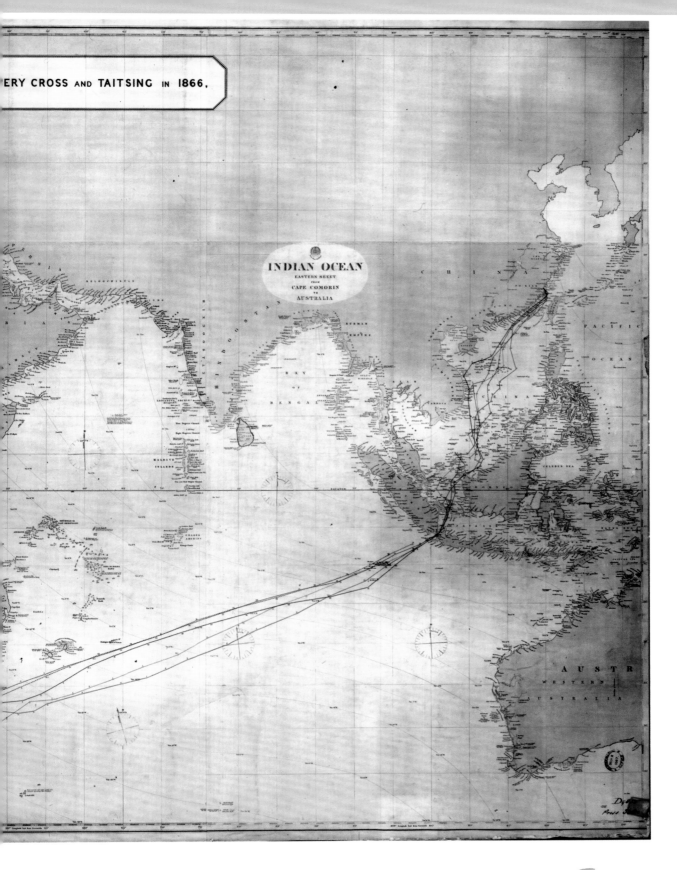

ERY CROSS AND TAITSING IN 1866,

INDIAN OCEAN
EASTERN SHEET
FROM
CAPE COMORIN
TO
AUSTRALIA

the chart

	Sail from Fou-chow-fou	Passed Anjer	Passed Mauritius	Passed C. of Good Hope	Passed St. Helena	Passed Ascension	Passed The Line	Passed Cape Verde I.s (St Antono)	Passed Azores (Flores)	Passed Entrance of English Channel	Arrived in The Downs
	May 30. 10.30 a.m	June 20 - 21	July 1 - 2	July 15 - 16	July 29 - 30	Aug. 1 - 2	Aug. 4 - 5	Aug. 10 - 11	Aug. 29 - 30	Sept. 4 - 5	Sept. 6. 8.0 a.m.
NG	May 30. 10.50 .	. 20 - 21	. 1 - 2	. 16 - 17	. 27 - 28	July 31 - Aug. 1	. 4 - 5	. 13 -14	. 29 - 30	. 4 - 5	. 6. 8.10 a.m.
A	May 30. 10.50 .	. 20 - 21	. 22 - 23	. 19 - 20	. 29 - 30	Aug. 2 - 3	. 6 - 7	. 13 -14	. 29 - 30	. 4 - 5	. 6. 12.45 noon
CROSS	May 29.	June 29 - 30	. 15 - 16	. 28 - 29	. 1 - 2	. 4 - 5	. 13 -14	. 29 - 30	. 5 - 6	. 7. during night
NG	May 31. Midnight	. 26 - 27	July 9 - 10	. 24 - 25	Aug. 5 - 6	. 8 - 9	. 12 - 13	. 19 - 20	Sept. 1 - 2	. 7 - 8	. 9. during night

CREDITS

I: The Aberdeen Clipper *Chrysolite*, engraving from *Illustrated London News*, author's private collection, courtesy of State Library of Victoria, Australia
II-III: The *Sobraon* Loading at Circular Quay, 1871, courtesy of State Library of Victoria

INTRODUCTION
VI: *Ariel* and *Taeping*, Charles Vickery, courtesy of marineoilpaintings.blogspot.com
VIII-IX: Clippers on the River Min, Richard Linton, courtesy of artist, www.lintonmaritimeart.com.au

CHAPTER ONE
X: Ship in Light Airs, Robert Salmon, courtesy of Sotheby's
2: Opium Ships off Lintin, 1824, William John Huggins, courtesy of Christie's
3: (top) The Opium Clipper *Sylph*, William John Huggins, courtesy of Sotheby's, (bottom) *Shenandoah*, Randon Rynd, courtesy of artist
4: (top) *America vs Maria*, Shane Couch, courtesy of artist, (bottom) *Malabar*, William Clark, courtesy of Yale Center for British Art
5: (top) *Oriental* Arriving in London Dock, George Campbell, courtesy of Adlard Coles Nautical, (bottom) *Oriental*, *Illustrated London News*, author's private collection
6: San Francisco, courtesy of Library of Congress
7: (top) USM Ship *Pacific*, Day and Son, (bottom left) The First Pan, (bottom right) Clipper Cards, all courtesy of Library of Congress
8-9: *Flying Cloud*, Richard Loud, courtesy of artist, www.maritimeartstudio.com
10: (top) Clipper *Robin Hood*, Samuel Walters, courtesy of Bonhams, (bottom) Golden Point, Ballarat, 1851, David Tulloch, courtesy of State Library of Victoria
11: (top) World Sailing Routes, David R MacGregor, courtesy of ss Great Britain Trust, (bottom) On the Bowsprit, *Daily Graphic*, courtesy of Marguerite Blanck Collection
12: (top) Tea Plant, unknown artist, author's collection, (bottom) *Sovereign of the Seas*, David Thimgan, courtesy of Vallejo Gallery, www.vallejogallery.com
13: Map of East Indies, Thomas Cary, courtesy of Geographicus Rare Antique Maps
14: Two Views of the *Ambassador*, Carlos Avalos, courtesy of artist
15: Lines plans of Atlantic Packet Ship, the US clipper *Witch of the Wave* and the *Titania*, David R MacGregor, courtesy of author's collection
16: The *Clyde*, unknown artist, courtesy of author's collection
17: (top) *Ariel*, Kay Jefferson, courtesy of artist, (bottom) Fate of the *Ariel*, George Campbell, courtesy of Adlard Coles Nautical
18-19: *Taeping*, D M Little, courtesy of State Library of Victoria
20: Ship *Thomas Reed* towing into San Francisco, David Thimgan, courtesy of Vallejo Gallery
21: *Flying Cloud*, Frederick Cozzens, author's collection

CHAPTER TWO
22: *Flying Cloud*, Richard Loud, courtesy of artist
24: Robert Waterman, unknown artist, courtesy of Solano County Library
25: (top) The *Sea Witch*, Richard Linton, courtesy of artist, (bottom) New York City Seen from Brooklyn, 1824, Baron Axel Leonhard Klinkowström, courtesy of Geographicus Rare Antique Maps
26-27: *Flying Fish* and *Wild Pigeon*, Richard Loud, courtesy of artist
28: (top) The Launch of the *Challenge*, George F Campbell, courtesy of Adlard Coles Nautical, (bottom) The Harbour of Boston with the City in the Distance, Fitz Henry Lane, courtesy of Cleveland Museum of Art
29: (top) *Flying Cloud*, Currier and Ives, courtesy of State Library of Victoria, (bottom) Boston Harbour, Fitz Henry Lane, courtesy of Kennedy Galleries Inc
30: (top) The Sail Plan of the *Challenge*, David R MacGregor, courtesy of ss Great Britain Trust, (bottom) *Challenge*, Antonio Jacobsen, courtesy of Bonhams
31: (top) Ship Passing Minot's light, Clement Drew, courtesy of Pierce Galleries, www.piercegalleries.com, (bottom) The *Golden State* Entering New York Harbour, Fitz Henry Lane, courtesy of Metropolitan Museum of Art
32: Semiramis Sailing Card, courtesy of Library of Congress
33: *Challenge*, LeBreton, author's private collection
34: (top) *Olivebank*, courtesy of State Library of Victoria, (bottom) Decks Awash, Richard Quiller Lane, author's collection
35: (top) *Loch Etive*, (bottom) *Garthsnaid*, both photographs courtesy of State Library of Victoria
36-37: *Flying Cloud*, James Buttersworth, private collection
38: *Flying Cloud* Approaching the Golden Gate, James Buttersworth, author's collection
39: (top) Ship at Sea, Marshall Johnson, courtesy of Pierce Galleries, (bottom) *Challenge* Arriving Off the Golden Gate, Shane Couch, courtesy of artist
40: *Young America*, photograph courtesy of Donald Dyal Collection
42-43: San Francisco View, unknown artist, courtesy of Library of Congress
44: San Francisco, Deserted Ships of the Gold Rush, 1849, John Stobart, courtesy of Kensington-Stobart Gallery, www.kensingtonstobartgallery.com
45: (top) Yerba Buena Cove 1849, courtesy of Library of Congress, (bottom) San Francisco Bay, 1850, author's collection
46: *Challenge* off the English Coastline, Samuel Walters, courtesy of Bonhams
47: Abandoned Ships, San Francisco, author's collection

CHAPTER THREE
48: *Marco Polo*, Montague Dawson, author's collection
50: (top) Melbourne 1854, unknown artist, courtesy of State Library of Victoria, (bottom) James Forbes, Kay Jefferson, courtesy of artist
51: (top) *Lightning under sail*, D M Little, courtesy of State

Library of Victoria, (bottom) Governor Ames Launch, courtesy of Maine Memory Network
52-53: *Marco Polo*, Thomas Robertson, courtesy of State Library of Victoria
54: Liverpool, Robert Salmon, courtesy of author's private collection
55: Ballarat Gold Fields, Samuel Thomas Gill, courtesy of State Library of Victoria
56: (top) Emigrants Embarking, (bottom) Rough Seas, *The Graphic*, both courtesy of Marguerite Blanck Collection
58-59: *Marco Polo*, D M Little, courtesy of State Library of Victoria
60: Ship off Penobscot Lighthouse, Clement Drew, courtesy of Pierce Galleries
61: (top) Hobsons Bay, courtesy of State Library of Victoria, (bottom) The *HMS Challenger* Off the Kerguelen Islands, *Illustrated London News*, author's private collection
62-63: *Red Jacket* in Ice, Currier and Ives, courtesy of Library of Congress
64-65: The *Kent, Lightning* and *Shalimar* at Hobsons Bay, Captain Thomas Robertson, courtesy of State Library of Victoria
67: (top) On Company Business, Jim Griffiths, courtesy of artist, (bottom) *Schomberg*, G H Andrews, courtesy of National Maritime Museum
68: (top) Final Goodbye, (bottom left) Life Aboard, *The Graphic*, courtesy of Marguerite Blanck Collection, (bottom right) *Schomberg* Satire, unknown artist, courtesy of State Library of Victoria
69: Ship in Ice, *Illustrated London News*, author's collection
70: (top) Cape Otway, Robert Bruce, courtesy of State Library of Victoria, (bottom) The *Schomberg* Fitting Out in Aberdeen Prior to her Maiden Voyage, courtesy of State Library of South Australia
72: The Wreck of the *Cromdale*, courtesy of State Library of Victoria
73: Ship at Sea, Alfred Jensen, Agra-Art, Warsaw
74-75: After the Storm, William Bradford, courtesy of Philadelphia Museum of Art
76: *Lightning*, courtesy of State Library of Victoria
77: (top) *Lightning*, Jan de Quelery, courtesy of artist, www.quelery.nl, (bottom) *Lightning* on Fire off Geelong, courtesy of the State Library of Victoria
78: Star of Peace, courtesy of State Library of Victoria
78: (top) Portland Showing the Ship *Frances Henty*, Thomas Robertson, courtesy of the State Library of Victoria, (bottom) *Lightning* arriving in Hobsons Bay, Richard Linton, courtesy of artist

CHAPTER FOUR
80: Ship off Cape Horn, unknown artist, courtesy of Library of Congress
82: Men in Rigging, *Garthsnaid*, Allan Green, courtesy of State Library of Victoria
83: *Invercauld* in Heavy Seas, courtesy of Donald Dyal Collection
84: (top) The Ships *Southern Cross* and *Winged Arrow* in Boston Harbour, Fitz Henry Lane, courtesy of Cincinnati Art Museum, (bottom) *Red Cloud*, courtesy of Donald Dyal Collection
85: Cape Horn, author's collection
86-87: The *Neptune's Car* in Chinese Waters, Kay Jefferson, courtesy of artist
88: (top) Delaware, Thomas Birch, courtesy of White House Historical Association, (bottom) Mary Patten, Kay Jefferson,

courtesy of artist
89: *Edward O'Brien*, David Thimgan, courtesy of Vallejo Gallery
90: Port Stanley, courtesy of Falkland Islands Tourist Board
91: Cape Horn, courtesy of National Oceanic and Atmospheric Administration
92: Valparaiso, artist unknown, courtesy of State Library of Victoria
93: (top) *Starlight* in Harbour, Fitz Henry Lane, courtesy of Nelson-Atkins Museum of Art, (bottom) San Francisco Docks, courtesy of Donald Dyal Collection
94-95: (top) *Abner Coburn*, courtesy of Donald Dyal Collection, (bottom) San Francisco View, courtesy of Library of Congress
96: San Francisco Quayside, courtesy of Donald Dyal Collection
98: (top) San Francisco, unknown artist, (bottom) Aerial View of San Francisco, Currier and Ives, courtesy of Library of Congress
99: *Flying Fish*, David Thimgan, courtesy of Vallejo Gallery
100-101: Boston Harbour, unknown artist, courtesy of Library of Congress

CHAPTER FIVE
102: *Dreadnought*, G M Gardner, courtesy of Jack Fine Art, www.jackfineart.com
104: (top) Samuel Samuels, courtesy of Library of Congress, (bottom) New York off Ailsa Craig, William Clark, courtesy of Yale Center of British Art
105: *A J Fuller* off San Francisco, David Thimgan, courtesy of Vallejo Gallery
106-107: *A J Fuller*, courtesy of Donald Dyal Collection
108: Dropping Off a Pilot, unknown artist, courtesy of Library of Congress
109 and 110: Passenger Muster, *The Graphic*, courtesy of Marguerite Blanck collection
111: Whaler and Fishing Vessels, William Bradford, courtesy of Indianapolis Museum of Art
112: *Abner Coburn*, 113: Panay, courtesy of Donald Dyal Collection
114-115: *Thomas Reed*, David Thimgan, courtesy of Vallejo Gallery
116: (top) Going Aloft, Henry Scott Tuke, courtesy of Trehayes Collection, (bottom) Eastern Point Light, Winslow Homer, courtesy of Princeton University Art Museum
117: *Jabez Howes*, courtesy of Library of Congress
118-119: New York, Currier and Ives, courtesy of Library of Congress
120: Bows of the *Dreadnought*, author's private collection
121: Ships at Sea 1867, Daniel Melbye, author's private collection
122: (top) Painting the Rudder, Henry Scott Tuke, courtesy of Trehayes Collection, (bottom) Rescue, courtesy of State Library of Victoria
123: (top) *Fleetwing, Henrietta* and *Vesta*, Currier and Ives, author's collection, (bottom) Smashed Wheel, courtesy of State Library of Victoria
124: Clipper Ship in a Hurricane, James Butters worth, courtesy of Bonhams
125: Deckhouse, Winslow Homer, courtesy of Princeton University Art Museum

CHAPTER SIX

126: *Ariel* and *Taeping*, Geoff Hunt, courtesy of Art Marine, www.artmarine.co.uk

128: (top) Pagoda Anchorage 1866, courtesy of State Library of South Australia, (bottom) Pagoda Anchorage, James Butt, courtesy of National Maritime Museum

129: Cultivating the Tea Plant, William Daniell, Yale Center for British Art

130: (top) *Serica*, D M Little, courtesy of State Library of Victoria, (bottom) Madras, or Fort St George in the Bay of Bengal – A Squall Passing Off, William Daniell, courtesy of Yale Center of British Art

131: (top) The Min River, courtesy of Creative Commons, (bottom) China River, unknown artist, author's collection

132: The *Fiery Cross*, George Campbell, courtesy of Adlard Coles Nautical

133: *Ariel*, John Fraser, courtesy of National Maritime Museum

134-135: *Ariel* and *Taeping*, D M Little, courtesy of State Library of Victoria

136: (top left) Captain John Keay, Kay Jefferson, courtesy of artist, (top right) Captain Donald MacKinnon, courtesy of An Iodhlann Museum, Tiree, (bottom) *Ariel*, *Illustrated London News*, courtesy of State Library of Victoria

137: Tea Advert, courtesy of State Library of Victoria

138: Ship in Gale, Allan Green, courtesy of State Library of Victoria

139: *Salamis*, courtesy of State Library of Victoria

140: (top) The Full Rigged Ship *Thomas Blythe* Signalling her Number off Whampoa, Chinese School, courtesy of Christie's, (bottom) Out on Stunsail Boom, courtesy of State Library of Victoria

141: (top) Chinese War Junk, unknown artist, courtesy of National Maritime Museum, (bottom) A Frigate in a Storm, James Buttersworth, courtesy of Pierce Galleries

142: (top) Men Aloft, Richard Quiller Lane, author's collection, (bottom) A Frigate in a Storm, James Buttersworth, courtesy of Pierce Galleries

144-145: Racing up the Atlantic, unknown artist, author's collection

146: (top) Fleeting Colours, the *Taitsing*, Jim Griffiths, courtesy of artist, (bottom) Pilot Cutter No. 3 Heading Back Inshore, with a Large Merchantman Hove-to Out in the Bay, Henry King Taylor, courtesy of Bonhams

147: Seascape, Alfred Meeres, author's collection

148-149: *Taitsing*, Chinese School, author's collection

150: Unloading Tea, *Illustrated London News*, courtesy of ss Great Britain Trust

151: (top) Journey's End, Henry Scott Tuke, courtesy of Bonhams, (bottom) Ship and Tug Negotiating a Price, David Thimgan, courtesy of Vallejo Gallery

152-153: The Needles, Edward Cooke, courtesy of Yale Center of British Art

154: A Packet Ship Under Sail in a Breeze off the South Foreland, Thomas Luny, courtesy of Yale Center of British Art

155: (top) Mist in Port, London, Charles de Lacy, courtesy of Bonhams, (bottom) *Lahloo*, courtesy of ss Great Britain Trust

156: Tea Race Notice, courtesy of ss Great Britain Trust

CHAPTER SEVEN

158: unknown clipper, Montague Dawson, courtesy of Sotheby's

160: Ship Sailing Down Channel, courtesy of ss Great Britain Trust

161: Coastal Scene, James Hamilton, courtesy of Bonhams

162: (top) *Sir Lancelot* Dismasted, George Campbell, courtesy of Adlard Coles Nautical, (bottom) *Loch Vennachar* Dismasted, courtesy of State Library of Victoria

163: Sir Lancelot, D M Little, courtesy of State Library of Victoria

164-165: Carrick Roads, Henry Scott Tuke, courtesy of Bonhams

166: (top) Captain Richard Robinson, Kay Jefferson, courtesy of artist, (bottom) *Maitland* Sail Plan, courtesy of ss Great Britain Trust

167: Map of the China Sea, courtesy of ss Great Britain Trust

168: Sailing Ship Under Way, courtesy of State Library of Victoria

169: *Sir Lancelot* Bow, George Campbell, courtesy of Adlard Coles Nautical

170: (top) *Sir Lancelot* and *Blackadder*, David Thimgan, courtesy of Butler Fine Art

170-171: (bottom) The Pagoda Anchorage, courtesy of State Library of South Australia

172: *Thermopylae*, Allan Green, courtesy of State Library of Victoria

173: (top) *Salamis*, Allan Green, courtesy of State Library of Victoria, (bottom) The *Thermopylae* and the *Cutty Sark*, Jan de Quelery, courtesy of artist

174: (top) View on the Pearl River, Macau, Eduard Hildebrandt, courtesy of Bonhams, (bottom) Hong Kong, *The Graphic*, courtesy of Marguerite Blanck Collection

175: (top) *Thermopylae*: Power and Grace, Jim Griffiths, courtesy of the artist, (bottom) *Sir Lancelot* in the China Sea, Thomas Dutton, author's collection

176: *Thermopylae*, D M Little, courtesy of State Library of Victoria

178: (top) *Spindrift*, *Illustrated London News*, courtesy of State Library of Victoria, (bottom) A Change in the Weather, Jim Griffiths, courtesy of artist

179: *L'Avenir*, courtesy of State Library of Victoria

180: *Thermopylae*, courtesy of ss Great Britain Trust

181: The Port of London, Thomas Luny, courtesy of Yale Center for British Art

182: (top) Suez Canal, author's collection, (bottom) *Ly-ee-Moon*, courtesy of State Library of Victoria

183: *Aldinga*, Thomas Robertson, courtesy of State Library of Victoria

CHAPTER EIGHT

184: *Cutty Sark* in the Roaring Forties, courtesy of Cutty Sark Trust

186: (top) *Cutty Sark* and *Thermopylae* Loading Tea, Donald Sinclair Swan, courtesy of Cutty Sark Trust, (bottom) Sleeping Sailor, Henry Scott Tuke, courtesy of Bonhams

187: *Illawarra*, Allan Green, courtesy of State Library of Victoria

188: (top) *Lahloo*, Jim Griffiths, courtesy of artist, (bottom) The Old Sea Dog, Henry Scott Tuke, courtesy of Bonhams

189: *Cutty Sark*, Allan Green, courtesy of State Library of Victoria

190: *Cutty Sark*, John Fraser, courtesy of National Maritime Museum
191: (top) *Loch Etive*, Allan Green, courtesy of State Library of Victoria, (bottom) Ship in Carrick Roads, Henry Scott Tuke, courtesy of Bonhams
192: *Cutty Sark*, unknown artist, courtesy of State Library of Victoria
194-195: *Cutty Sark* and *Thermopylae* racing, unknown artist, courtesy of State Library of Victoria
196: (top) *Blackadder*, Allan Green, courtesy of State Library of Victoria, (bottom) The *Cutty Sark*'s Jury Rudder, courtesy of ss Great Britain Trust
197: *Halloween*, Allan Green, courtesy of State Library of Victoria
198: (top) Ships in Melbourne, Allan Green, (bottom) *Thessalus*, Pelham Jones, courtesy of State Library of Victoria
199: *Salamis* and *Loch Maree*, Allan Green, courtesy of State Library of Victoria
200-201: Port Jackson, Conrad Martens, courtesy of Art Gallery of New South Wales
202: *Cutty Sark* at Circular Quay, Allan Green, courtesy of State Library of Victoria
203: Windjammer in Falmouth Roads, Henry Scott Tuke, courtesy of Bonhams
204: A barque in an Estuary, Henry Scott Tuke, courtesy of Bonhams
205: (top) *Cutty Sark*, (bottom) *Cutty Sark* Loading at Circular Quay, Allan Green, both courtesy of State Library of Victoria

206: *Brilliant* and *Thermopylae*, Allan Green, courtesy of State Library of Victoria
207: (top) *Cutty Sark* Hove to Awaiting a Pilot, courtesy of Cutty Sark Trust, (bottom) The Port Jackson, David Thimgan, courtesy of Vallejo Gallery
208: *Argonaut*, Jack Spurling, courtesy of Bonhams
209: (top) *Sardomene*, Pelham Jones, (bottom) Fort Macquarie, Robert Russell, courtesy of State Library of Victoria
210-211: *Cutty Sark* Drying Sails, Allan Green, courtesy of State Library of Victoria

EPILOGUE
212: *Titania*, courtesy of State Library of Victoria
214-215: Ships in San Francisco, courtesy of Donald Dyal Collection
215: (bottom) Barque Leaving Hamburg, unknown artist, author's collection
216: *Glory of the Seas*, Jan de Quelery, courtesy of artist
217: The *Aristides*, 218: Loading Wool, 219: The Miltiades, all courtesy of State Library of Victoria
220: The *Mountstewart*, courtesy of State Library of Victoria

APPENDIX
223: Clipper Ship *Maitland*, Jan De Quelery, courtesy of the artist
224-225: Chart of 1866 China Race, courtesy of United Kingdom Hydrographic Office

INDEX

Ambassador 14
America, yacht 4, 6
Anjer 166, 189, 193, 203–4
Ariel VIII–IX, 16–17, 127, 129, 132–7, 140, 143, 147, 150, 154, 156–7, 161, 163, 166, 171, 176–7, 179, 190, 213, 216, 223–5

Baines, James, ship owner 10, 55, 57, 60, 66, 69, 73, 214
Baltimore clippers 2–3
Black Ball Line 49, 55, 57–9, 77, 104, 108, 214
Blackadder 170, 196, 204
Boston 10, 28–9, 32, 60, 66, 84, 92, 100–1, 221–2
Bruce, Captain of the *Cutty Sark* 196–7, 199, 202–4, 206

Cape of Good Hope 20, 55, 69, 147, 169, 178–80, 183, 197
Cape Horn 6, 10, 21, 34–7, 40–1, 44, 60, 66, 81–3, 85, 88–92, 99, 101, 125, 213, 216–8
Challenge 28–47, 214
China Sea 13, 16, 133, 137, 141, 143, 163, 166–8, 172, 175, 179, 202–03, 216, 221
China tea race
    1866 127–157, 161, 223–5
    1867 166–70, 222
    1869 VIII, 166, 171–83, 222
Cutty Sark 20, 185–211, 217–9, 222

Dana, Richard Henry 6, 90
Douglass, Jim, mate of the *Challenge* 33, 38, 40–1, 44, 46–7
Dreadnought 103–25

Fiery Cross 127–9, 132–3, 137, 140, 143–5, 147, 150, 156–7, 166, 168, 171, 217, 223–5
Flying Cloud 7–9, 20–3, 29, 32–3, 35–8, 41, 47, 66, 89, 214, 221
Flying Spur VII, 128, 169
Forbes, James 'Bully' 49–51, 55, 57, 60, 66–71, 73, 76, 79

gold rush
    Australian 10, 12
    Californian 6, 23, 28, 41, 44–5, 94–5, 98
Griffiths, John W, designer 1–2

Halloween 197, 222
Houqua 2

icebergs 69, 71, 81, 111
Innes, George 127, 129, 137, 154, 157, 171, 178, 180, 216–7

James Baines 10, 108, 222

Keay, John 20, 132–3, 136–7, 150, 154, 157, 163, 166, 177, 216

Keeler, William, mate of the *Neptune's Car* 89–92, 97, 99
Kemball, Robert 177, 179–81, 183, 217

Lightning 10, 49–51, 60–7, 71, 73–7, 79, 216, 222
Liverpool VII, 10, 33, 49, 51, 54–5, 57, 60, 66–7, 69, 76, 103–4, 109–10, 163, 216, 222
Lochleven Castle VII
London 5–6, 55, 89, 127, 129, 132, 137, 150, 155–7, 177, 181, 190, 206, 210–1, 222–3

McKay, Donald, shipbuilder 7, 10, 32–3, 47, 60, 89, 99, 216
MacKinnon, Donald 127, 136–7, 143, 150, 154, 157, 216
Maitland 163, 166, 170, 223
Marco Polo 49, 51–60, 66, 76, 216
Mary Patten 81–101
Melbourne 49–50, 57, 60–1, 64–6, 69–71, 79, 177, 198–9, 210, 222
mutiny 33, 38, 46, 103, 111, 120–1, 203

Natchez 24
Neptune's Car 81–101, 216
New York 1–2, 4, 6–7, 23–8, 31–2, 66, 83, 89, 99–100, 103–4, 108, 112, 118–21, 125, 190, 203–4, 206, 221
NL&G Griswold, owners of *Challenge* 23, 29, 32, 46
Nutsford, Captain 132, 137

opium clippers 2–3
Oriental 5

packet rats 33, 103–4, 109
Pagoda anchorage 127–9, 131-2, 170–3, 179–80
Patten, Joshua 85, 89–92, 97, 99–101

Rainbow 1–2
Rapid 83, 85, 91–2, 99, 101
record passages 5–10, 24–5, 28–9, 32, 57, 66, 69, 89, 108, 177, 179–81, 183, 221–2
Red Jacket 61–3, 66, 222

River Min VIII–IX, 129, 131, 155, 163, 172
Robin Hood 10
Robinson, Richard 127, 129, 132–3, 143, 147, 150, 157, 159–183, 217

Salamis 137, 139, 173, 199, 202
Samuels, Samuel 103–25
San Francisco 6–7, 12, 20, 26–9, 32–3, 35, 38–9, 40–7, 66, 83, 85, 89–92, 94–9, 112, 125, 221
Schomberg 49, 66–73, 76, 79, 216
Sea Witch 6, 24–5, 28, 32
Serica VIII–IX, 127, 129–30, 132–3, 137, 143, 147, 154, 157, 163, 171, 176, 190, 216–7, 223–5
Sir Lancelot 159–83, 217, 222
Smith, James, builder of the *Marco Polo* 51, 55
Sovereign of the Seas 12, 221
Spindrift 171, 176, 178, 180–1, 190, 216
Steele, Robert, shipbuilder 17, 132–5, 155, 188
Suez Canal 20, 182–3, 197
Sydney 78–9, 177, 199–202, 206–7, 209–11, 219, 222

Taeping 17–9, 127–30, 132–6, 143, 147, 154–7, 163, 176–7, 190, 216, 222–5
Taitsing 128, 132–3, 137, 143, 146-9, 157, 217
Thermopylae VIII–IX, 16, 20, 166–7, 171–3, 175–7, 179–81, 183, 186, 193–7, 202, 206–7, 210–11, 213, 217, 219, 222
Titania 14–15, 143, 190, 193, 213, 217, 222

Valparaiso 92, 97

Wallace, Richard 188–91, 193, 197, 203
Waterman, Robert 23–47, 57, 214
Willis, Jock, owner of the *Cutty Sark* 193, 196–7, 204, 206, 211
wool trade 20, 73, 173, 206, 210, 217–9

Acknowledgements

Given that a large portion of this book is filled with many beautiful images, I am indebted to a range of people for their patience and kindness in helping me source so many. First up, I'd like to thank Mary MacLean and the wonderfully picturesque museum of Ad Iodhlann on the Scottish Island of Tiree for her kindness and diligence in helping me source pictures and information on Donald MacKinnon and his ship, *Taeping*. Her efforts went well beyond anything I could have expected. Secondly, I need to thank artists Jim Griffiths, Jan de Quelery, Richard Linton, Richard Loud and Shane Couch for patiently sending through many images and also June Carey, widow of David Thimgan, for her co-operation in allowing me access to his many beautiful paintings. I also need to thank the Vallejo Gallery in San Francisco for supplying me with the images. Marguerite Blanck was also exceedingly helpful in supplying me with many etchings from the *Graphic* journal. I also owe the Cutty Sark Trust a debt of gratitude and the same goes for the SS Great Britain Trust for their kindness in letting me access their David R MacGregor collection. I also include a number of images by the late George Campbell. I have made every effort to contact his family to gain their consent, but have failed, so apologies to any members of his family. Lastly, I would like to thank my mother, Kay Jefferson, who kindly painted a number of pictures which appear in the book and also my girlfriend Ivory who spent many long evenings patiently listening to me reading back endless drafts.